# Knitting

## IN·STYLE

A YARNWORKS KNITTING BOOK

# Knitting

## IN · STYLE

**30** ORIGINAL HAND-KNITTING DESIGNS

Collins 8 Grafton Street, London W1X 3LA

A YARNWORKS KNITTING BOOK

First published in Great Britain
in 1987 by
William Collins Sons & Co Ltd
London · Glasgow · Sydney
Auckland · Toronto ·
Johannesburg

Designed by Janet James
How-to-knit Illustrations by June
Tiley

ISBN 0 00 412187 2

Typeset by Ace Filmsetting, Ltd,
Frome, Somerset
Originated in Hong Kong by
Bright Arts (HK) Ltd
Printed and bound in Singapore
by Tien Wah Press (Pte) Ltd

# Contents

## ACKNOWLEDGEMENTS

Yarnworks Ltd would like to thank the following people
who have helped to make this book special:
Photography: Tony McGee
Make up: Carol Langbridge and Barbara Daly using
'Colourings from Barbara Daly', a Body Shop product
Hair: Rene Gelston and Thomas McIver
Stylist: Linda McClean
All the models
A special thank you is due to all our hardworking
sample knitters, to Eve White, and to
Janet James and Caroline White at Collins.

# *Introduction*

About ten years ago the fashion world was set alight by a new generation of British knitwear designers who produced original hand knitted sweaters that were bought by well dressed women everywhere.

Since then hand knitting has been popularized by the growing number of people who realized that they could make their own designer knitwear at a fraction of shop prices. Handknits have now become an essential fashion item, part of everybody's wardrobe.

This book contains thirty stylish designs by Suzanne Russell, who has achieved international recognition for exclusive designer knitwear. They are all surprisingly easy to knit, and will make you feel great when you wear them. They are modern classics, for women, men and children, for all four seasons of the year, for day and evening wear, for town and country.

You cannot create a special sweater from second rate ingredients, which is why at Yarnworks we only spin our wool from Merino fleeces. The Merino sheep is the aristocrat of the sheep world and produces wool which is both soft and durable. We then hank-dye this wool to produce exactly the right fashion shades. With Yarnworks patterns and yarns you will be able to make sweaters that will feel as expensive as they look.

We are sure you will enjoy knitting the sweaters in the book, and once you make your first one we think you'll be hooked.

Steven Grant
*Yarnworks*

## CASTING ON

There are three basic methods of casting on stitches:
a) The thumb method – using one needle.
b) The chain edge – casting on with two needles.
c) The cable edge – casting on with two needles for a firmer edge.

**The thumb method**
Make slip loop in the yarn about 90 cm (36 in) from the end (a). (This length varies with the number of stitches to be cast on – 90 cm (36 in) will cast on about one hundred stitches. A guide to the length required is: the width of the piece of knitting to be cast on, multiplied by three.) Wrap the yarn round your left thumb and grasp the yarn firmly between your palm and fingers, making a loop (a). Insert the needle into this loop (b). Now wrap the yarn round the needle (c) and draw it

through the loop on your thumb (d). As you slip the loop from your thumb, gently tighten the left-hand thread (e). You have now formed the first stitch. Repeat the process for the rest of the row.

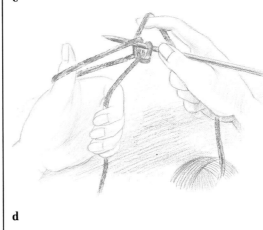

c

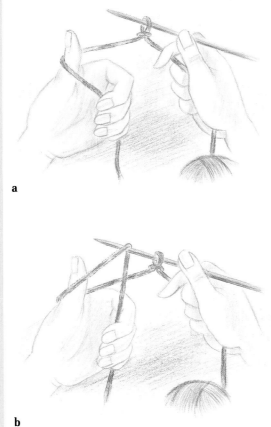

a

d

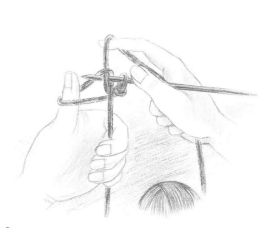

b

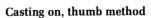

e

**Casting on, thumb method**

## The chain edge

This method is used when a loose edge is required. For a slightly tighter and more elastic edge, knit through the back of each stitch on the following row. On the left-hand needle, make a loop as given in diagram a of the thumb method. Hold the yarn and second needle in the right hand. Place right needle through loop, wind yarn round the needle and draw through, making a new loop. Put this loop on left needle to make a second stitch. Continue thus until required number of stitches have been cast on.

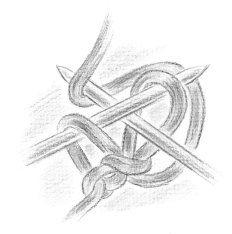

**Chain edge casting on**

## The cable edge

The same principle applies as for chain edge casting on, except that the right needle is placed *between* two stitches instead of *through* one stitch. This gives a firm elastic edge and is suitable for most thicker yarns. The first loop is on left needle. Make a second stitch then insert the right needle point between the stitches to make the next stitch. Continue thus for required number of stitches.

**Cable edge casting on**

## CASTING OFF

This is the procedure for fastening off the stitches when the knitting has been finished. The stitches can be knitted, purled or worked off in a pattern.

With the work on the left-hand needle, begin by knitting two stitches at the beginning of the row. With yarn at back of work, pick up second stitch with point of left needle and slip it over first stitch, leaving one stitch on right hand needle. Knit another stitch from left needle, making two stitches again on right needle. Lift the first over the second as before.

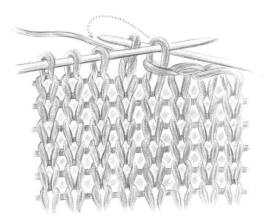

**Casting off**

Continue in this way until the last stitch remains. Break yarn, pass it through this stitch, pull up and fasten off.

## TENSION

Before starting to knit any garment you should make a tension sample in the yarn to be used, to measure the stitch gauge. Using the yarn, needles and stitch pattern stated, knit a sample slightly more than 10 cm (4 in) square. Lay the finished sample on a flat surface without stretching it. With pins mark out the tension measurements given in the instructions. If there are too few stitches in your piece of knitting for the stated tension measurement, then your knitting is too loose. Try again with a smaller needle. If there are too many stitches for the stated tension measurement, then your knitting is too tight. In this case try a size larger needle. Use whichever needles give you the correct tension.

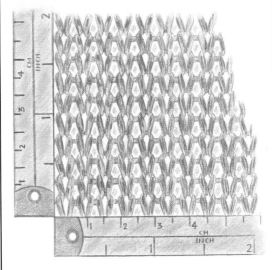

**Checking tension**

## CORRECT MEASURING

It is most important to work to the correct measurements whenever they are given in the instructions. Place the knitting on a flat surface and measure it on the straight grain.

## BASIC STITCHES – KNIT (K), PURL (P)

These two stitches are the basis for all knitted fabrics. Patterns are constructed from a combination of these two stitches.

### Knit

The needle which holds the cast-on stitches should be in the left hand. With the yarn behind the work, insert right needle through first stitch on left needle from front to back and pass yarn round and under needle point. Draw loop through stitch, at the same time slipping stitch off left needle. Continue thus until all the stitches are on the right-hand needle.

### Purl

The needle which holds the cast-on stitches should be in the left hand. With the yarn in front, insert right needle through first stitch from back to front. Pass yarn round point of needle, over the top and then under. Draw loop through stitch on left needle, at the same time slipping the stitch off left needle. The new stitch is now on right needle. Continue thus until all stitches are on the right-hand needle.

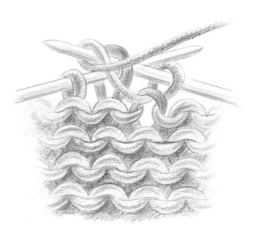

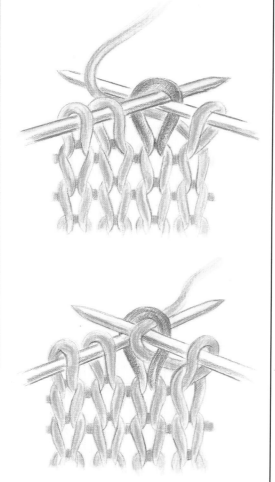

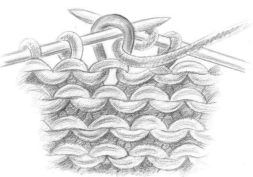

**How to knit a stitch**

**How to purl a stitch**

## SIMPLE INCREASING

When shaping garments it is necessary to make extra stitches. These can be added at either end of the needle as on sleeves or sides, or they can be added evenly across the row.

### Increasing on a knit row

Knit into the front of the stitch in the usual way, leaving the actual stitch still on the left needle. Then knit into the back of it, thus making two stitches from the one.

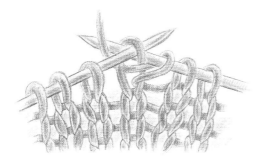

**Knit increasing**

### Increasing on a purl row

Purl into the front of the stitch in the usual way, leaving the stitch still on the left needle. Then purl into the back of it, slipping both stitches off needle together.

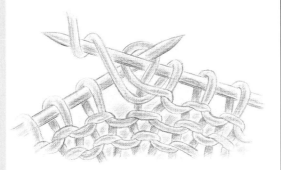

**Purl increasing**

## SIMPLE DECREASING

When it is necessary to decrease stitches for shaping, the simplest way is to knit two stitches together, or purl two stitches together at the beginning or end, or at any point along the row. In a knit row the decrease forms a slant to the right if the stitches are knitted together through the front, and a slant to the left if knitted together through the back.

### Decreasing in a knit row

Place right-hand needle through the front of the first two stitches on left needle front to back. Knit them together as a single stitch.

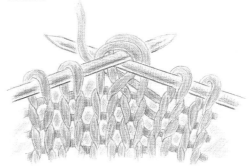

**Decreasing knitways**

### Decreasing in a purl row

Place the right-hand needle through the front of the first two stitches on left-hand needle back to front. Purl them together as a single stitch.

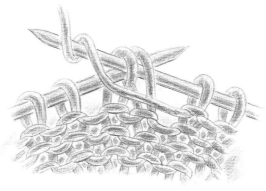

**Decreasing purlways**

If other forms of decreasing are used in this book they are given under the individual patterns.

## PICKING UP STITCHES ROUND ARMHOLES AND NECK EDGES AND UP FRONTS

Unless care is taken, holes and irregular stitches will appear round edges where stitches are not picked up correctly. This could spoil the look of a finished garment. It is better, for picking up the stitches, to use a size smaller needle than the size to be used for the actual neckband or border – this will avoid stretching the stitches and will give a neater edge. Stitches are always picked up with the right side of the work facing you.

When picking up stitches through a straight cast-off edge, pick them up through both loops. When picking up stitches along a shaped edge which has been decreased, the edge will be uneven with long and short stitches at the edge. In this case, pick up two stitches through the long loops and omit the short loops, to get an even edge.

When picking up stitches up a straight side (a front edge) then pick up both loops of the stitch.

## BUTTONHOLES

There are three basic ways of making a buttonhole. When using fine yarn or making a small garment where the buttonholes will be very small, the simplest method on a knit row is to work to the position of the buttonhole then, yarn forward, knit two stitches together. On a purl row work to the position of the buttonhole then, yarn round needle, purl two stitches together.

### A horizontal buttonhole

The usual way of making one is worked as follows: knit or purl to the position of the buttonhole, cast off the required number of stitches for size of button, work to end of row. On the next row, work to the cast off stitches, then cast on by the Thumb Method the same number of stitches, then work to end of row. On the next row pick up the loose thread at the corner of the buttonhole, work the next stitch, then pass the picked up stitch over. This gives a firm neat buttonhole.

### A vertical buttonhole

Sometimes a vertical buttonhole is preferable, then in this case work as follows: work to the position of the buttonhole, then divide the stitches between the two needles. For the left-hand needle you will need to introduce some new yarn as shown. Work an equal number of rows on the two sets of stitches with another set of needles to correspond with the size of the button, ending on the wrong side of both sets of stitches. On the next row work across both sets of stitches.

## HOW TO PICK UP DROPPED STITCHES

If you drop a stitch from your needle, there is a simple way to pick it up.

**Picking up on a knit row**
Pick up the stitch and the strand above it on the right needle from front to back. Insert left needle through the stitch only from back to front. Then with right needle pull the loop through the stitch to make the new stitch on right needle, at the same time dropping stitch from left needle. Transfer the remade stitch on to left needle so that it can now be knitted.

**Picking up on a purl row**
Pick up the stitch and the strand above it on the right needle from back to front. Place left needle through stitch only from front to back. Then with right needle, pull the loop through the stitch to make the new stitch, at the same time dropping stitch from left needle. Transfer the stitch on to left needle, ready for purling.
If a knit stitch has dropped several rows down, it is easier to use a crochet hook and hook up one strand at a time to remake the stitch, pulling the strand through the front of the stitch. Continue until each strand has been hooked up. With a dropped stitch on a purl row, put the hook through the back of the dropped stitch and pull the strand through the back each time. Continue until each strand has been hooked up.

## COLOUR BLOCK KNITTING

Blocks or bands of colour are usually worked on a stocking stitch fabric of one row knit and one row purl. Introduce the contrast colours where indicated and remember to twist the two yarns round each other on the wrong side of the work to avoid holes. Separate balls of yarn should be used for each block of colour. To prevent tangling, keep each colour on a separate bobbin or use small balls of each colour and slip an elastic band over each to prevent them unwinding.

## FAIR ISLE KNITTING

This usually consists of knitting with two colours at a time; one colour in the right hand and the other in the left. Knit the colour in the right hand in the usual way, holding the other colour free at the back. To knit with the second colour, pull a loop of the second colour through the stitch at the required position. Continue knitting holding the second colour in the right hand and the first colour free in the left.
The carrying of the colour not in use is called 'stranding'. A colour should not be carried over more then three or four stitches as it will give too long a strand. If it has to be carried over more stitches then weave it over and under the colour that is being used.

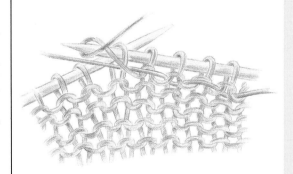

**Weaving colours**

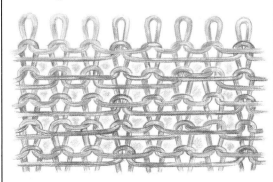

**Stranding colours**

## CHARTS AND HOW TO READ THEM

Most Fair Isle and colour pattern designs are worked from a chart which saves a great deal of space and gives a clearer picture of what the design looks like than written instructions. Most Fair Isle designs are worked in stocking stitch – therefore all odd-numbered rows on the chart, unless otherwise stated, are knit rows and all even-numbered rows are purl rows.

Knit rows are worked from right to left of the chart and purl rows are worked from left to right.

Each symbol on the chart represents a colour which is given in the key. Each square on the chart represents one stitch and one row.

The chart gives one repeat of the pattern. The number of stitches in the repeat should divide into the number of stitches in the row, unless there are extra stitches at either end, in which case it will be indicated on the chart.

The numbers printed at the sides of the chart are the rows which make up the pattern repeat.

## SWISS DARNING

This embroidery, used to decorate knitted fabrics, is sometimes known as Knitting Stitch. It is worked on stocking stitch with each embroidered stitch directly over a knitted stitch.

Thread a blunt-ended tapestry needle with the yarn used in the knitting. Bring the needle up through the centre of the stitch from back of work, insert from right to left behind stitch immediately above. Now take needle down through centre of first stitch and out through centre of next stitch to the left.

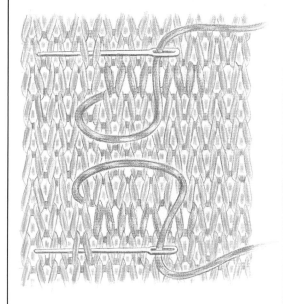

**Swiss darning**

## MAKING UP

Begin by blocking the garment. Place the knitted sections right side down on a folded towel or thick ironing blanket and pin out the corners to the correct measurements. Cover the knitting with a clean cloth (dry or damp, according to the instructions given on the ball-band). Press lightly with a warm iron, lifting the iron off the knitting between each press. Do not go over the knitting with a pushing movement and never press the ribbing.

### Back stitch seam

Most garments are made up with a back stitch seam which gives a tailored finish. Use the same yarn or matching plain yarn if the yarn used has bobbles or an uneven bulky twist. Split the strands of thicker yarns to avoid too heavy a seam. Place the two pieces of knitting evenly together (wrong sides outside) and pin in position. Sew together with a row of narrow back stitch, worked one stitch in from the edge.

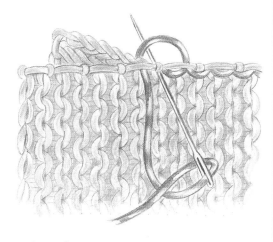

Back stitch seaming

### Flat seam

This is used when sewing very thick or heavily textured garments. Place the two edges together with right sides facing. Sew backwards and forwards through the two thicknesses just through the edge, taking care to match rows on the two pieces.

### Invisible seam

Place two edges side by side, right sides uppermost. Join yarn to right-hand edge, pick up stitch just opposite on left-hand edge. Pick up stitch in row above on right-hand edge; pull yarn through and tighten. Continue in this way, going from edge to edge, pulling the yarn through and tightening it after each stitch until the seam is finished. Fasten off.

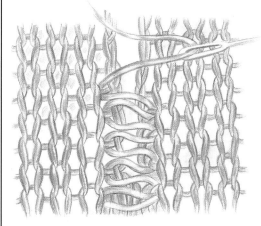

Invisible seaming

## SEWING IN ZIPS

Great care must be taken when sewing in zips. Too often a zip is eased into an opening; the result is a wavy fastening instead of a flat, almost invisible one.

Match length of zip carefully with the length of the opening. Pin zip in position on wrong side of fabric, easing in the fabric slightly rather than the zip. Take care that the top ends are folded nearly inside. Tack in place with small running stitches close to the teeth of the zip, then oversew all round edge with tiny stitches in matching cotton.

## GRAFTING

This can be used as an alternative to casting off if a flat invisible seam is required. Divide the stitches of the two edges to be joined equally on two needles. Place side by side, one in front of the other, wrong sides inside. Thread a length of yarn, long enough to work across the row, through a blunt-ended tapestry needle.
* Put tapestry needle knitways through stitch on front needle, draw yarn through stitch and slip off needle. Put tapestry needle through next stitch on front needle purlways, pull yarn through but let stitch stay on needle. Place yarn under needle and thread through first stitch purlways into first stitch on back needle; bring yarn through and slip stitch off needle. Put tapestry needle knitways into next stitch on back needle, draw yarn through but let stitch stay on needle. Bring yarn forward under needle. *
Repeat from * to * until all stitches have been worked off.

## HOW TO MAKE CASING FOR AN ELASTIC WAISTBAND

Cut elastic to fit waist comfortably and join into a circle. Lay the elastic in position round waistband on wrong side. With a crochet hook and yarn, work a zig-zag crochet casing as follows: begin at side seam. Work a slip stitch into lower edge of waist ribbing, make the required number of chain stitches to fit the width of the elastic, then make a slip stitch into top edge of waist ribbing. Continue until casing fits all round elastic. Fasten off.

## HOW TO SHORTEN OR LENGTHEN A GARMENT BY PULLING A THREAD

This needs to be done with great care but it means that you will only need to re-knit the ribbing if the garment has stretched in wear. It can either be lengthened by knitting downwards and then knitting the ribbing, or shortened by unravelling some of the rows and then knitting the ribbing. Begin by opening the side seams of ribbing. With a sharp pair of scissors carefully cut the head of one stitch near the end of the row just above the ribbing. Now carefully separate the rib from the main work as you go, cutting the same strand at intervals to facilitate the separation of the two pieces of knitting.

## USING A CIRCULAR NEEDLE

This is a flexible nylon tube which has two pointed metal ends. These are sized as ordinary needles and can be bought in lengths from 40 to 100 cm. Use one needle point to cast on stitches on to the other point in the usual way. When the required number of stitches has been cast on, join them into a round by transferring the left-hand point to the right-hand point and vice versa. Knit the first cast-on stitch using the working yarn from the right-hand point. Continue using the right-hand point to knit off the stitches until the round is completed. Mark the beginning of rounds with a contrast marker. Remember that the outside of the work will always face you, so that if knitting stocking stitch, you simply knit every round.

# BASIC *Knitting* TECHNIQUES

## WASHING AND DRYING INSTRUCTIONS

It is essential that you follow the washing and drying instructions on the ball bands of all the yarns you use. If washing is permitted, then hand washing is always best. For yarns made mainly of wool, use warm water, and a warm rinse. Squeeze moisture out with garment wrapped in towels, then *dry flat* after carefully patting the garment into the required size and shape. Be sure that the ribbing, cuffs and neckband ribs are not stretched but pushed together to retain their shape and elasticity. Do not dry in direct heat (radiators or fires). Do not dry white handknits in direct sunlight.
For yarns made with acrylic it is important to rinse in cold water and if you spin-dry use the short cycle.

## CHOICE OF YARN

Each pattern has been specifically written for the Yarnworks yarn stated.
Alternative yarns will prove unsuitable. Yarn quantities are based on average requirements and are therefore approximate. It is not advisable to buy less than stated in the instructions as colours cannot always be matched.

## SIZES

Where garments are more than one size the smallest size is given first with larger sizes following on.

## ABBREVIATIONS

**k** – knit; **p** – purl; **st(s)** – stitch(es); **tog** – together; **alt** – alternate; **beg** – beginning; **foll** – following; **cont** – continue; **rep** – repeat; **rem** – remain(ing); **patt** – pattern; **inc** – increase (by working into front and back of the next st); **dec** – decrease (by working 2 sts tog.); **sl** – slip; **psso** – pass slipped st over; **yb** – yarn back; **yf** – yarn forward; **yrn** – yarn round needle; **tbl** – through back of loop(s); **skpo** – slip 1, k1, pass slipped stitch over; **st st** – stocking stitch (k on right side and p back); **rev st st** – reversed stocking stitch (p on right side and k on back); **g st** – garter stitch (k on every row); **m-st** – moss stitch (kl and pl alternately and on subsequent row the stitches are reversed); **k1 below** – knit next st through row below; **KFB (or PFB)** – knit (or purl) into front and back of next st; **wyrn** – wind yarn round needle number of times stated in pattern; **mm** – millimetres; **cm** – centimetres; **in** – inch(es); **g** – gramme; **ndl(s)** – needle(s); **M or MC** – main colour; **C** – contrast; **0** – no stitches worked in that particular size.
**Note:** Always join yarn at side seams.

## NEEDLE CONVERSIONS

| UK and Australian metric | Original UK and Australia, Canada, S. Africa | USA |
|---|---|---|
| 2 mm | 14 | 00 |
| 2¼ mm | 13 | 0 |
| 2¾ mm | 12 | 1 |
| 3 mm | 11 | 2 |
| 3¼ mm | 10 | 3 |
| 3¾ mm | 9 | 4 |
| 4 mm | 8 | 5 |
| 4½ mm | 7 | 6 |
| 5 mm | 6 | 7 |
| 5½ mm | 5 | 8 |
| 6 mm | 4 | 9 |
| 6½ mm | 3 | 10 |
| 7 mm | 2 | 10½ |
| 7½ mm | 1 | 11 |
| 8 mm | 0 | 12 |
| 9 mm | 00 | 13 |
| 10 mm | 000 | 15 |

## AMERICAN TERMINOLOGY

Most knitting terms are identical in English and American usage. The exceptions to this are listed below, with the English term used in the book.

Stocking stitch (st st)=stockinette stitch; yarn round needle (yrn)=yarn over needle (yon); cast off=bind off; double crochet (DC)=single crochet; tension=gauge.

Knitting
PATTERNS

# Prairie

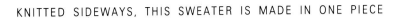

## Stitches used
Mainly in stocking stitch with pleat and neckband in reverse stocking stitch. Welt and cuffs two-and-two rib.

## Sizes
Small/medium – to suit bust sizes 86/91 cm (34/36 in); length from shoulder 56 cm (22 in); sleeve seam 39 cm (15½ in).

## Materials
Ten/eleven 50g balls of Yarnworks French Poodle shade 1703; plain matching yarn for sewing up. The quantities of yarn specified are based on average requirements and are therefore approximate.

## Needles
8 mm (no. 0) and 15 mm.

## Tension
6½ sts and 9½ rows to 10 cm (4 in) square over stocking stitch on 15 mm ndls.

## Note
Sweater is knitted sideways in one piece beginning at left sleeve edge. Where there is one set of figures this applies to both sizes.

## Instructions

### MAIN PART

With 8 mm ndls, cast on 22 sts.
*Row 1*: (right side) K2, (p2,k2) to end.
*Row 2*: P2, (k2,p2) to end.
Rep these 2 rows until rib measures 6 cm (2½ in) from cast-on edge, ending with row 2.
Change to 15 mm ndls. Cont in st st, beg with a k row, inc 1 st inside the first and last st on 5th and every foll 6th row, 6 times in all. 34 sts. Next row p.

### Shape for back and front
Cast on 7 sts at beg of next 4 rows. 62 sts. Work a further 16.5/18 cm (6½/7 in) straight.

### Shape neck
*Next row*: K 31 sts and leave these sts on a spare ndl, k2tog and k to end.

### FRONT NECK

Cont on last set of sts and dec 1 st at neck edge on 2 foll alt rows. 28 sts. Work 5 rows straight.

### Make pleat
Work 6 rows in reverse st st, beg with a p row. With wrong side of work facing and using 8 mm ndl, pick up 28 sts along the first row of reverse st st.
With right side of work facing and using 15 mm ndl, k to end knitting tog 1 st from each ndl.
Work 5 rows in st st, beg with a p row. Inc 1 st at neck edge on next and 2 foll alt rows, 31 sts.
Next row p.
Leave these sts on a spare ndl.
With wrong side of work facing, rejoin yarn to sts on first spare ndl. Work 21 rows in st st, beg with a p row.
*Next row*: K to end then k across sts on spare ndl. Work 16.5/18 cm (6½/7 in) straight, ending with a p row.
Cast off 7 sts at beg of next 4 rows.

### Shape sleeves
Dec 1 st inside the first and last st on next row and every foll 6th row, 6 times, 22 sts.
Work 5 rows straight.
Change to 8 mm ndls.
Work 6.5 cm (2½ in) in rib as given for left cuff. Cast off in rib.

### FRONT NECKBAND

With right side of work facing and using 8 mm ndls, pick up and k 20 sts along front neck. Work 4 rows in reverse st st, beg with k row. Cast off.

### BACK NECKBAND

With right side of work facing and using 8 mm ndls, pick up and k 18 sts along back neck. Work 4 rows in reverse st st, beg with a k row. Cast off.

### WELTS

With right side of work facing and using 8 mm ndls, pick up and k 46/50 sts along lower front edge. Work 7.5 cm (3 in) in rib as given for left cuff, beg and ending with row 2.
Cast off in rib.
Work back welt in same way.

## To Make Up

Do not press. Join lower sleeve and side seams using plain matching yarn and a fine back stitch. Join short sides of neckband using a flat seam. Allow to curl under.

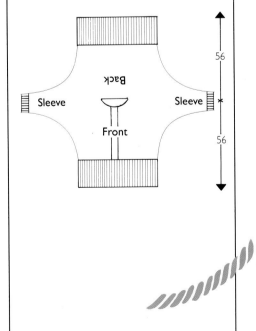

## Stitches used

Mainly in stocking stitch. Two-and two rib for welts, cuffs and collar.

## Sizes

Small/medium/large – to suit bust 86/91/96 cm (34/36/38 in); length from shoulder about 66/66/66 cm (26/26/26 in).

## Materials

Twelve/thirteen/thirteen 50g balls of Yarnworks French Poodle, shade 1702; matching thread to join seams.
The quantities of yarn specified are based on average requirements and are therefore approximate.

## Needles

6 mm (no. 4), 10 mm (no. 000), circular ndls 6½ mm (no. 3) and 7½ mm (no. 1) for collar; st-holder.

## Tension

9 sts and 12 rows to 10 cm (4 in) square measured over stocking stitch on 10 mm ndls.

## Note

Instructions given for three sizes.

## Instructions

### FRONT AND BACK

(Worked in one piece.)
Begin at lower edge of front and with 6 mm ndls cast on 38/40/42 sts.
Work 9 cm (3½ in) in k2, p2, rib, ending right-side rows with k2 and wrong-side rows with p2 on small and large sizes and dec 1 st at each end of last row on all sizes. 36/38/40 sts.

Change to 10 mm ndls.
Work 6 rows in st st, then inc 1 st at each end of next row and every foll 4th row, until there are 50/52/54 sts.
Work one row straight.

### Shape for sleeves

Cast on 2 sts at beg of next 12 rows, 3 sts at beg of foll 4 rows and 5 sts at beg of next 2 rows. 96/98/100 sts.
Work 10 rows straight.

### Divide for neck

*Next row* (right side): K42/43/44, slip next 12 sts onto a st-holder for centre front neck, then k the rem 42/43/44 sts.
Cont on last set of 42/43/44 sts.
*Next row*: P.
** Cast off 2 sts at beg (neck edge) of next row and foll alt row. 38/39/40 sts.
Work 3 rows straight. ***
Leave these sts on a spare ndl.
Rejoin yarn to neck edge of rem 42/43/44 sts and p to end of row.
Knit one row back to neck edge, then rep from ** to *** on first side.
Now join the two sets of sts tog and work the back as follows:
*Next row* (right side): On to ndl holding the 38/39/40 sts of left shoulder just worked, cast on 20sts for back of neck, then on to same ndl k38/39/40 sts of right shoulder from spare ndl. 96/98/100 sts.
Work 17 rows straight in st st, beg with a p row.

### Shape for sleeves

Cast off 5 sts at beg of next 2 rows, 3 sts at beg of foll 4 rows and 2 sts at beg of next 12 rows. 50/52/54 sts.
Now dec 1 st at each end of next row and every foll 4th row until 36/38/40 sts rem.
Work 7 rows straight, increasing 1 st at each end of last row. 38/40/42 sts.
Change to 6 mm ndls.
Work 9 cm (3½ in) in k2, p2 rib, ending right-side rows with k2, and wrong-side rows with p2 for small and large sizes.
Cast off in rib.

### COLLAR

With 6½ mm circular ndl pick up and k 8 sts down left side of front neck, k 12 sts from st-holder at centre front neck, pick up and k 8 sts up right side of front neck, then pick up and k 20 sts along back of neck. 48/48/48 sts.
*Inc round*: K and inc 4 sts evenly. 52/52/52 sts.
Now work in k2, p2 rib until collar measures 6.5 cm (2½ in) from beg.
*Next round*: * K1, k twice into next st p2; rep from * all round. 65/65/65 sts.
*Next round*: * K3, p2; rep from * all round. Cont in rib as now set until collar meassures 19 cm (7½ in) from beg.
*Next round*: * K2, k twice into next stitch p2, rep from * all round. 78/78/78 sts.
Change to 7½ mm circular ndl and cont in rib for a further 2.5 cm (1 in).
Cast off loosely in rib.

### CUFFS

With 6 mm ndls and right side of work facing pick up and k 28 sts along row ends of sleeve edge. Work 7.5 cm (3 in) in k2, p2 rib. Cast off in rib.

## To Make Up

Do not press. Join side and sleeve seams, using matching thread and a fine backstitch.

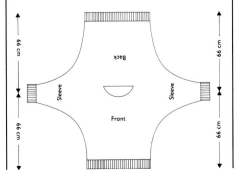

# Winter Sports

## Stitches used

Mainly in stocking stitch with panels of cable and reversed stocking stitch. Two-and-two rib for welts, cuffs and neckband.

## Sizes

Extra small/small/medium/large – to suit bust 81/86/91/97 cm (32/34/36/38 in); length from shoulder 61/66/66/66 cm (24/26/26/26 in); sleeve seam 43/44.5/45.5/47 cm (17/17½/18/18½ in).

## Materials

Fourteen/fifteen/sixteen/seventeen 50g balls of Yarnworks Merino Sport. The quantities of yarn specified are based on average requirements and are therefore approximate.

## Needles

4½ mm (no. 7); 5½ mm (no. 5); a set of four double-pointed 4½ mm (no. 7) and 5 mm (no. 6) ndls for the neckband; cable needle; st-holder.

## Tension

17 sts and 21 rows to 10 cm (4 in) square measured over stocking stitch on 5½ mm ndls.

## Special abbreviations

C13B – cable 13 back thus: slip next 6 sts on to a cable ndl and leave at back of work, k7, then k6 from cable ndl; C11B – cable 11 back thus: slip next 5 sts on to a cable ndl and leave at back of work, k6, then k5 from cable ndl; K1BW – knit into top of loop below thus making a stitch.

## Instructions

### BACK

With 4½ mm ndls cast on 90/96/100/104 sts.
Work in rib for 10 cm (4 in) as follows:
*Extra small size only:*
*Row 1* (right side): P2, * k2, p2; rep from * to end.
*Row 2*: K2, * p2, k2; rep from * to end.
*All other sizes:*
*Row 1* (right side): * K2, p2; rep from * to end.
*Row 2*: * P2, k2; rep from * to end.
Cont for all sizes as follows:
Change to 5½ mm ndls and work in st st until back measures 35.5/39.5/39.5/39.5 cm (14/15½/15½/15½ in) from cast-on edge, ending with a p row.

### Shape armholes

Cast off 9 sts at beg of next 2 rows. 72/78/82/86 sts.
Cont straight in st st until back measures 61/66/66/66 cm (24/26/26/26 in) from cast-on edge, ending with a p row.

### Shape shoulders

Cast off 12/14/15/16 sts at beg of next 2 rows, then cast off 12/13/14/15 sts at beg of foll 2 rows. Leave rem 24/24/24/24 sts on a spare ndl.

### POCKET LININGS (make 2)

With 4½ mm ndls cast on 24 sts.
*Medium size only:* K2, p2, rib.
*All other sizes:* P2, k2 rib.
Work in rib for 7.5 cm (3 in). Leave these sts on a spare ndl.

### FRONT

With 4½ mm ndls cast on 96/100/104/108 sts.
*All sizes:* Work in k2, p2 rib for 10 cm (4 in).
*1st pocket row* (right side):

K6/6/8/10, cast off 24 sts ribwise for pocket opening, (1 st on ndl), k9/11/11/11, p4, (K1BW – see special abbreviations – k1) 5 times, k3, p4, k10/12/12/12, cast off 24 sts ribwise for pocket opening, (1 st on ndl k5/5/7/9. 101/105/109/113 sts.
Change to 5½ mm ndls.
*2nd pocket row:* P6/6/8/10, p across the 24 pocket lining sts from spare ndl in place of those cast off on previous row, p10/12/12/12, k4, p13, k4, p10/12/12/12, then p across second pocket lining from spare ndl in place of those cast off on previous row, p6/6/8/10.
Now set sts for centre cable panel as follows:
*Row 1* (right side): K40/42/44/46, p4, k13, p4, k40/42/44/46.
*Row 2*: P40/42/44/46, k4, p13, k4, p40/42/44/46.
Rep rows 1 and 2 twice more.
*Row 7*: K40/42/44/46, p4, C13B – see special abbreviations – p4, k40/42/44/46.
*Row 8*: As row 2.
*Rows 9 to 20*: Rep rows 1 and 2 six times more.
These 20 rows set patt. Rep them until front measures 35.5/39.5/39.5/39.5 cm (14/15½/15½/15½ in) from cast-on edge, ending with a wrong-side row.

### Shape armholes

Keeping patt correct cast off 9 sts at beg of next 2 rows. 83/87/91/95 sts.
Cont straight in patt until front measures 54.5/58.5/58.5/58.5 cm (21½/23/23/23 in) from cast-on edge, ending with a wrong-side row.

### Shape neck

*Row 1*: K31/33/35/37, p3, k2 tog tbl, (k2 tog) 4 times, k3, k2 tog tbl, p3, k to end. 77/81/85/89 sts.
*Row 2*: P31/33/35/37, k1, turn; leaving rem 45/47/49/51 sts on spare ndl.
Cont on first set of 32/34/36/38 sts thus:

**\*\*Right half front**

Dec 1 st at neck edge of next row and every foll row until 25/27/29/31 sts rem.

Cont straight until front measures 61/66/66/66 cm (24/26/26/26 in) from cast-on edge, ending at armhole edge.

**Shape shoulder**

Cast off 13/14/15/16 sts at beg of next row.

Work one row, then cast off.

Return to the 45/47/49/51 sts left on a spare ndl and with wrong side of work facing slip the centre 13 sts on to a st-holder for the centre front neck.

With wrong side of work facing rejoin yarn at neck edge to rem 32/34/36/38 sts and work thus: K1, p to end of row.

**Left half front**

Work from \*\* on right half front to end.

### SLEEVES (both alike)

With 4½ mm ndls cast on 40/44/44/48 sts. Work in k2, p2 rib for 6.5 cm (2½ in) and inc 1 st at end of last row. 41/45/45/49 sts.

*Next row:* K13/15/15/17, p4, (K1BW, k1) 4 times, k3, p4, k to end. 45/49/49/53 sts.

Change to 5½ mm ndls.

*Next row:* P13/15/15/17, k4, p11, k4, p to end.

Now inc and work in patt as follows:

*Row 1* (right side): Inc into first st, k12/14/14/16, p4, k11, p4, k to last st, inc into last st.

*Row 2*: P14/16/16/18, k4, p11, k4, p to end.

*Row 3*: K to centre 19 sts, p4, k11, p4, k to end.

*Row 4*: Inc into first st, p to centre 19 sts, k4, p11, k4, p to last st, inc into last st.

*Row 5*: K to centre 19 sts, p4, C11B – see special abbreviations – p4, k to end.

*Row 6*: P to centre 19 sts, k4, p11, k4, p to end.

Cont as now set, working sts at each side of the 19 centre panel sts in st st and work a cable over centre 11 sts on every 18th row from previous cable row, still increasing 1 st at each end of every 3rd row foll previous inc row, until there are 97/101/101/103 sts, working extra sts in st st as they are made.

Cont straight in patt until sleeve measures 43/44.5/45.5/47 cm (17/17½/18/18½ in) from cast-on edge (measuring over centre cable panel), ending with a wrong-side row.

**Shape top**

Cast off 17/18/18/18 sts at beg of next 3 rows.

*Next row:* Cast off 17/18/18/18 sts, (1 st on ndl), p4/4/4/5, k3, p2 tog tbl, (p2 tog) 3 times, p3, p2 tog, k3, p to end.

Cast off.

### NECKBAND

Join shoulder seams, using a fine backstitch.

With right side of work facing slip first 6 sts from st-holder at centre front of neck onto a spare ndl.

With right side facing and with set of four double-pointed 4½ mm ndls join yarn at centre front and k2, p2, k2, p1 across the 7 sts from st-holder, then pick up and k20/22/24/26 sts up neck edge of right half front, k across the 24 sts from back neck, then pick up and

k21/23/25/27 sts down neck edge of left half front and finally k2, p2, k2 across centre sts left on spare ndl. 78/82/86/90 sts.

Turn and work in rows as follows:

*Row 1*: \* P2, k2; rep from \* to last 2 sts, p2.

*Row 2*: \* K2, p2; rep from \* to last 2 sts, k2.

Rep rows 1 and 2 twice more.

Change to 5 mm ndls and work rows 1 and 2 three times more.

Cast off in rib.

*To Make Up*

Do not press. Measure 5 cm (2 in) down from cast-off edge of sleeve and mark with pins. Set in sleeves, placing the row ends above the pins to cast-off sts at armholes. Join sleeve and side seams, using a fine backstitch.

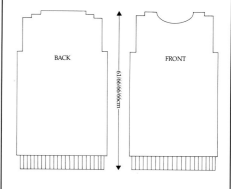

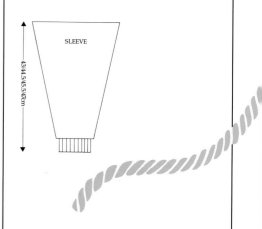

# Blue Chip

## Stitches used
Mainly in reverse st st with cables; welts, neckband and armbands in k1, p1 rib.

## Sizes
To fit bust 81–86(91–97/102–107/ 112–117) cm (32–34/36–38/40– 42/44–46 in); actual size 86/99/112/124 cm (34/39/44/49 in); full length 62/64/64/65 cm (24½/25/25/25½ in).

## Materials
Nine/nine/ten/ten 50g balls of Yarnworks Merino Sport. The quantities of yarn specified are based on average requirements and are therefore approximate.

## Needles
4½ mm (no. 7), 5½ mm (no. 5); a set of 4½ mm (no. 7) pointed both ends. Cable needle.

## Tension
17 sts and 21 rows to 10 cm (4 in) measured over stocking stitch on 5½ mm (no. 5) ndls.

## Special abbreviations
C9 – (cable 9 by slipping next 4 sts on to cable needle and leave at back of work, k5 then k4 from cable needle); M1 – (make one stitch by picking up thread between st just worked and next st and purl into back of it).

29

## Instructions

### FRONT

With 4½ mm ndls cast on 71/81/91/101 sts.
*Row 1*: (right side) K1, * p1, k1, rep from * to end.
*Row 2*: P1, * k1, p1, rep from * to end.
These 2 rows form rib.
Cont in rib until work measures 7.5 cm (3 in), ending with row 1.
*Inc row*: Rib 7/3/8/13, M1, * rib 3/4/4/4, M1; rep from * to last 7/2/7/12 sts, rib to end. 91/101/111/121 sts.
Change to 5½ mm ndls and patt.

*Row 1*: (Right side) P5, * k1 tbl, p3/4/5/6, k9, p3/4/5/6; rep from * to last 6 sts, k1 tbl, p5.
*Row 2 and every alt row*: K5, * p1 tbl, k3/4/5/6, p9, k3/4/5/6, rep from * to last 6 sts, p1 tbl, k5.
*Row 3*: As row 1.
*Row 5*: P5, * k1 tbl, p3/4/5/6, C9, p3/4/5/6; rep from * to last 6 sts, k1 tbl, p5.
*Row 7*: As row 1.
*Row 9*: As row 1.
*Row 11*: As row 1.
*Row 12*: As row 2.
These 12 rows form patt.

Cont in patt until work measures 33 cm (13 in) from beg, ending with a wrong side row.

#### Divide for neck
*Next row*: Patt 41/46/51/56, cast off next 9 sts, patt to end.
*Next row*: Patt 41/46/51/56, turn. Leave rem sts on a spare needle.
Keeping patt correct work 6 rows, dec 1 st at neck edge in next row and foll alt row 1/2/2/2 times more. 39/43/48/53 sts.

#### Shape armholes
*Next row*: K2 tog, patt to end.
*Next row*: Cast off 4 sts, patt to end.
Work 4/5/6/7 rows dec 1 st at neck edge on 3rd/1st/1st/1st row and every foll alt row 0/2/2/3 times more, at the same time dec 1 st at armhole edge on every row. 29/30/34/37 sts.
*3rd and 4th sizes only*:
Work 6/13 rows dec 1 st at neck edge only on 1st/2nd row and foll 2/5 alt rows. 31/31 sts.

### FOR ALL SIZES

Cont in patt dec 1 st at neck edge only on 3rd/4th/3rd/3rd row and every foll 4th row 11/10/9/7 times more. 17/19/21/23 sts.
Cont straight until armhole measures 25/27/27/28 cm (10/10½/10½/11 in) from beg, ending with a wrong side row.
Cast off.
With wrong side facing rejoin yarn to rem sts and patt to end.
Complete to correspond with first side of neck, reversing all shapings.

### BACK

Work as front until work measures same as front to armholes, ending with a wrong side row.

#### Shape armholes
Keeping patt correct, cast off 4 sts at beg of next 2 rows. Dec 1 st at each end of next 4/5/6/7 rows. 75/83/91/99 sts.
Cont straight until work measures same as front, ending with a wrong side row.

#### Shape shoulders
Cast off 17/19/21/23 sts at beg of next 2 rows.
Leave rem 41/45/49/53 sts on a spare needle.

### NECKBAND

Sew shoulder seams.
With right side facing and set of 4½ mm ndls pick up and k55/58/58/63 sts evenly from right of front neck, k41/45/49/53 sts from back neck and pick up and k55/58/58/63 sts evenly from left side of front neck.
Beg with row 2 work 4 cm (1½ in) in rib as given for front, ending row 2.
Cast off in rib.

### ARMHOLE BANDS

With right side facing and 4½ mm ndls, pick up and k105/109/113/117 sts evenly all round armhole edge.
Beg with row 2 work 4 cm (1½ in) in rib as given for front, ending row 2.
Cast off in rib.

## To Make Up

Placing right side over left side sew side edges of neckband together and sew to cast off sts at centre front. Sew side and armhole band seams.

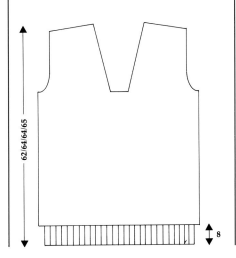

# Snowdrop

## Stitches used

Mainly in stocking stitch and knot and arrow pattern. Welts, neck and sleeve edgings in stocking stitch and reversed stocking stitch.

## Sizes

Medium/large – to suit bust 91 to 97/97 to 101 cm (36 to 38/38 to 40 in); length from shoulder about 61 cm (24 in); sleeve seam 43 cm (17 in).

## Materials

Eleven/twelve 50g balls of Yarnworks Merino Luxury Wool, shade 801; two small buttons. The quantities of yarn specified are based on average requirements and are therefore approximate.

## Needles

3¼ mm (no. 10) circular needle for neckband, 4½ mm (no. 7), 3¾ mm (no. 9); st-holder; medium size crochet hook.

## Tension

22 sts and 28 rows to 10 cm (4 in) square measured over stocking stitch on 4½ mm ndls.

## Note

Instructions given for two sizes.

## Special abbreviations

Knot 1 – made thus: all into next st work (k1, p1, k1, p1 and k1) then pass 4th, 3rd, 2nd and 1st st over the last st made; M1k – make 1 knit (by picking up horizontal bar lying between ndls and work into front of it; do not work into back of this loop as it will spoil the pattern).

## Instructions

### BACK

With 3¾ mm ndls cast on 95/99 sts using thumb method.
Work in ridge patt for welt as follows:
Row 1: (right side) P.
Row 2: K.
Row 3: P.
Row 4: P.
Rep rows 2, 3 and 4 once more.
Row 8: K.
Row 9: K.
Row 10: P.
Row 11: K.
Row 12: K.
Row 13: P.
Row 14: P.
Rep rows 12, 13 and 14 once more.
Row 18: K.
Inc row: K7/3, (inc into next st, k3) 22/24 times. 117/123 sts.
Change to 4½ mm ndls and work in main patt as follows:
Row 1 and foll 6 alt rows: (wrong side) P.
Row 2: K1/4, * skpo, k6, (M1k – see special abbreviations – k1) twice, sl.1, k2 tog, psso, (k1, M1k) twice, k6, k2 tog; ** rep from * to ** to last 1/4 sts, k1/4.
Row 4: K1/4, * skpo, k5, M1k, k1, M1k, k2, sl.1, k2 tog, psso, k2, M1k, k1, M1k, k5, k2 tog; ** rep from * to ** to last 1/4 sts, k1/4.
Row 6: K1/4, * skpo, k4, M1k, k1, M1k, knot 1 – see special abbreviations, k2, sl.1, k2 tog, psso, k2, knot 1, M1k, k1, M1k, k4, k2 tog; ** rep from * to ** to last 1/4 sts, k1/4.
Row 8: K1/4, * skpo, k3, M1k, k1, M1k, knot 1, k3, sl.1, k2 tog, psso, k3, knot 1, M1k, k1, M1k, k3, k2 tog; ** rep from * to ** to last 1/4 sts, k1/4.
Row 10: K1/4, * skpo, k2, M1k, k1, M1k, knot 1, k4, sl.1, k2 tog, psso, k4, knot 1, M1k, k1, M1k, k2, k2 tog; ** rep from * to ** to last 1/4 sts, k1/4.
Row 12: K1/4, * skpo, (k1, M1k) twice, knot 1, k5, sl.1, k2 tog, psso, k5, knot 1, (M1k, k1) twice, k2 tog,

** rep from * to ** to last 1/4 sts, k1/4.
Row 14: K1/4, * skpo, M1k, k1, M1k, knot 1, k6, sl.1, k2 tog, psso, k6, knot 1, M1k, k1, M1k, k2 tog, ** rep from * to ** to last 1/4 sts, k1/4.
These 14 rows form main patt.
Rep them 6 times more and the first row again. Back should now measure about 39.5 cm (15½ in) from cast-on edge.

## Shape armholes

Next row: Cast off 5 sts, (1 st on ndl) k4/7, M1k, k1, sl.1, k2 tog, psso, (k1, M1k) twice, k6, k2 tog, now rep from * to ** on patt row 2 to last 1/4 sts, k1/4.
Next row: Cast off 5 sts, p to end of row.
Next row: K2 tog, k4/7, sl.1, k2 tog, psso, k2, M1k, k1, M1k, k5, k2 tog, now rep from * to ** on patt row 4 to last 19/22 sts, then skpo, k5, M1k, k1, M1k, k2, sl.1, k2 tog, psso, k4/7, k2 tog.
Next row: P2 tog, p to last 2 sts, p2 tog.
Next row: K2 tog, k1/4, sl.1, k2 tog, psso, k8, k2 tog, now rep from * to ** on patt row 6 to last 16/19 sts, then skpo, k8, sl.1, k2 tog, psso, k1/4, k2 tog.
Next row: P2 tog, p to last 2 sts, p2 tog.
Next row: K2 tog, k9/12, now rep from * to ** on patt row 8 to last 11/14 sts, k9/12, k2 tog.
Next row: P2 tog, p to last 2 sts, p2 tog.
Next row: K2 tog, k7/10, now rep from * to ** on patt row 10 to last 9/12 sts, k7/10, k2 tog. 85/91 sts.
Purl one row.
Cont straight in patt beg with row 12, but keeping 8/11 sts at each end in st st, instead of 1/4 sts – row 12 will therefore read: k8/11, then rep from * to ** to last 8/11 sts, k8/11.
When back measures 61 cm (24 in) from cast on edge, cast off straight across taking tog every 9th and 10th st.

## FRONT

Work as given for back until front measures 56 cm (22 in) from cast on edge, ending with a wrong-side row.

**Shape neck**
*Next row:* Patt 31/34, turn leaving the rem 54/57 sts on a st-holder.
**\*\*** *Left half front*
Cont on first set of sts and dec for neck by casting off 2 sts at beg (neck edge) of next row and foll 5 alt rows. 19/22 sts.
Work 2 rows straight. Cast off.
Return to the rem 54/57 sts and with right side of work facing slip centre 23 sts on to a st-holder for centre front neck, rejoin yarn to rem 31/34 sts at neck edge.
*Right half front*
Work from \*\* on left half front to end.

## SLEEVES (both alike)

With 3¾ mm ndls cast on 44 sts, using thumb method as shown.
Work the 18 rows of ridge patt as given for welt on back.
*Inc row:* K and inc 5 sts evenly across row. 49 sts.
Change to 4½ mm ndls and work centre panel in main patt as given for back with 13 sts at each end in st st, as follows:
*Row 1 and foll 6 alt rows:* P.
*Row 2:* K13, then work from \* to \*\* once on main patt row 2 then, k13.
*Row 4:* K13 then work from \* to \*\* once on main patt row 4 then, k13.
*Row 6:* K13, then rep from \* to \*\* once on main patt row 6, then k13.
*Row 8:* K13, then work from \* to \*\* once on main patt row 8, then k13.
*Row 10:* K13, then work from \* to \*\* once on main patt row 10, then k13.
*Row 12:* K13, then work from \* to \*\* once on main patt row 12, then k13.
*Row 14:* K13, then work from \* to \*\* once on main patt row 14, then k13.

These 14 rows set patt for sleeves.
Cont as now set and inc 1 st at each end of next row and every foll 6th row, until there are 75 sts, working the extra sts into st st as they are made.
Work straight until sleeve measures 43 cm (17 in) from cast on edge, ending with a wrong-side row.

**Shape top**
Cast off 3 sts at beg of next 2 rows, then dec 1 st at each end of next row and every foll alt row until 43 sts rem, after which dec 1 st at each end of every foll row until 17 sts rem. Cast off.

## NECKBAND

First join shoulder seams, using a fine backstitch.
Mark centre back of neck with a coloured thread.
With 3¼ mm circular ndl begin at coloured marker at centre back of neck and with right side facing pick up and k19 sts across left back of neck. 14 sts down left side of front neck, 23 sts from st-holder at centre front neck, pick up and k14 sts up side of right front neck and 19 sts along right back neck. 89 sts. Remove marker.
Work in rows as follows:
*Row 1:* (wrong side) K.
*Row 2:* P.
*Row 3:* P.
*Row 4:* K.
Rep rows 2, 3 and 4 once more.
*Row 8:* K.
*Row 9:* P.
*Row 10:* K.
*Row 11:* K.
Rep rows 2, 3 and 4 twice more.
*Row 18:* K.
*Row 19:* P.
*Row 20:* K.
*Row 21:* K.
*Row 22:* P.
Cast off knitwise.

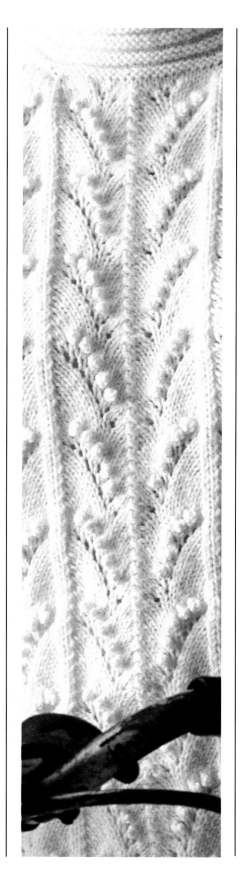

35

# To Make Up

Do not press. Set sleeves into armholes, then join sleeve and side seams, using a fine backstitch. Using crochet hook work a row of double crochet down right side of back neck opening.

On left side of back neck opening work 2 rows of double crochet, working 2 button loops at equal intervals. Sew on 2 buttons to left back opening to correspond with button loops.

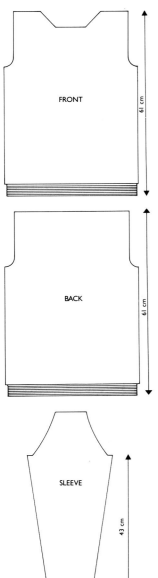

FRONT

61 cm

BACK

61 cm

SLEEVE

43 cm

## Stitches used
Mainly in stocking stitch; two-and-two rib for welts, cuffs and collar.

## Sizes
Small/medium/large – to suit bust 86/91/97 cm (34/36/38 in); length from shoulder 68.5/68.5/70 cm (27/27/27½ in).

## Materials
Eleven/twelve/thirteen 50g balls of Yarnworks French Poodle, shade 1706; two shoulder pads; matching thread to join seams. The quantities of yarn specified are based on average requirements and are therefore approximate.

## Needles
6 mm (no. 4), 5 mm (no. 6), 10 mm (no. 000).

## Tension
9 sts and 12 rows to 10 cm (4 in) square measured over stocking stitch on 10 mm ndls.

## Note
Instructions given for three sizes.

### Instructions

### FRONT AND BACK

(Worked in one piece)
Begin at the lower edge of the front and with 6 mm ndls cast on 42/44/46 sts.
Work in k2, p2 rib for 23 cm (9 in), ending right-side rows with k2, and wrong-side rows with p2 on small and large sizes.
Change to 10 mm ndls.
*Dec row:* (wrong side) P2/4/1, * p2 tog, p6/6/7; rep from * to end. 37/39/41 sts.
Cont in st st and work 8 rows straight, then inc 1 st at each end of next row and every foll 4th row, until there are 43/45/47 sts.
Purl one row, then inc 1 st at each end of next row and every foll alt row until there are 49/51/53 sts. Purl one row.

### Shape sleeves
Inc 1 st at each end of every row until there are 65/69/73 sts.
Now cast on 3 sts at beg of next 2 rows, 4 sts at beg of foll 4 rows and 8 sts at beg of next 2 rows. 103/107/111 sts.
Now divide sts for neck thus:
*Next row:* K47/49/51 sts, cast off 9 sts for centre front neck, k to end of row.
Cont on last set of 47/49/51 sts for Right side of neck thus:
Dec 1 st at neck edge on next 5 rows. 42/44/46 sts.
Work 6 rows, then cast on 19 sts for back of neck. Leave these 61/63/65 sts on a spare ndl.

### Left side of neck
Rejoin yarn at neck edge of the 47/49/51 sts for left side of neck and dec 1 st at neck edge on the next 5 rows. 42/44/46 sts.
Work 6 rows straight.
*Next row:* K the left side of neck sts, then onto same ndl k across the 61/63/65 sts left on spare ndl. 103/107/111 sts. Cont across all sts and work 11 rows straight in st st.

### Shape sleeves
Cast off 8 sts at beg of next 2 rows, 4 sts at beg of next 4 rows, 3 sts at beg of foll 2 rows, after which dec 1 st at each end of every foll row until 49/51/53 sts rem.
Now dec 1 st at each end of every foll alt row until 43/45/47 sts rem.
Work 3 rows straight, then dec 1 st at each end of next row and every foll 4th row until 37/39/41 sts rem.
Work 7 rows straight.
*Inc row:* P2/4/1, * inc into next st, p6/6/7; rep from * to end. 42/44/46 sts.
Change to 6 mm ndls.
Work in k2, p2 rib as for Front for 23 cm (9 in).
Cast off in rib.

### CUFFS
With 6 mm ndls and right side of work facing pick up and k 28 sts evenly along row ends of sleeves.
Work in k2, p2 rib for 6.5 cm (2½ in).
Cast off in rib.

### COLLAR
With 5 mm ndls cast on 76 sts.
Work 7 rows in k2, p2 rib.
Cast off in rib.

### To Make Up
Do not press. Join sleeve and side seams, using matching thread and a fine backstitch. Join row ends of collar, then sew to neck edge, placing seam at centre back neck. Sew in shoulder pads.

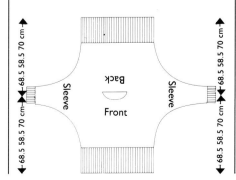

# Autumn Leaves

PERFECT TWEEDY CARDIGAN FOR AN AUTUMN AFTERNOON

## Stitches used

Mainly in open-work leaf pattern on a rev.st st background. One-and-one rib for welts, cuffs, front bands and neckband.

## Sizes

Small/medium – to suit bust 86/91 cm (34/36 in); length from shoulder 59.5/59.5 cm (23½/23½ in); sleeve 43/43 cm (17/17 in).

## Materials

Nine/ten 50g balls of Yarnworks Donegal Tweed Wool in Slate, shade 905 (main colour) and one/one 50g ball of Yarnworks Merino Luxury Wool in each of the following colours: 817, 818, 820; 8 small buttons; two shoulder pads. The quantities of yarn specified are based on average requirements and are therefore approximate.

## Needles

3¼ mm (no. 10), 4 mm (no. 8).

## Tension

24 sts and 26 rows to 10 cm (4 in) square measured over reversed stocking stitch on 4 mm ndls.

## Special abbreviations

M1k – make 1 knit (by picking up loop that lies between st just worked and following st and k into back of it); M1p – make 1 purl (as M1k but purl into back of st); SSK – slip stitches knitwise (slip next 2 sts knitwise one at a time, then insert point of left-hand ndl into the fronts of these 2 sts and k them tog in this position).

## Instructions

### LEAF PATTERN

**Note**

Instructions given for two sizes. Follow the diagram for the position of the coloured leaves. Work the coloured leaves where indicated on the right of the main stem beg on rows 2 to 24 the sts are underlined with a straight line. The coloured leaves where indicated on the left side of the main stem beg on rows 13 to 24 and continue from 1 to 12 the sts have been underlined with a wavy line. The remainder of the leaves are worked in MC in pattern. Use separate balls of yarn for each coloured leaf and do not pass the MC across back of coloured leaves, but join on another ball of MC to work the other side, joining in and breaking off the yarns as required. Twist the yarns round each other when changing colour to avoid a hole.

Where a number of sts is given this refers to the basic number and does not include those made in patt.

*Row 1* (wrong side): K1, p1, * k5/6, p5, k4, p3, k9/10, p2, **; rep from * to ** 3 times more, ending last rep with p1, k1, instead of p2.
*Row 2*: K2, * p7/8, p2 tog, M1k – see special abbreviations – k3, p4, k2, M1k, k1, M1k, k2, p5/6, k2, **; rep from * to ** 3 times more.
*Row 3*: K1, p1, * k5/6, p7, k4, p2, k1, p1, k8/9, p2, **; rep from * to ** 3 times more, ending last rep with p1, k1, instead of p2.
*Row 4*: K2, * p6/7, p2 tog, k1, PFB, k2, p4, k3, M1k, k1, M1k, k3, p5/6, k2, **; rep from * to ** 3 times more.
*Row 5*: K1, p1, * k5/6, p9, k4, p2, k2, p1, k7/8, p2, **; rep from * to ** 3 times more, ending last rep with p1, k1, instead of p2.
*Row 6*: K2, * p5/6, p2 tog, k1, PFB, p1, k2, p4, yb, SSK – see special abbreviations – k5, k2 tog, p5/6, k2, **; rep from * to ** 3 times more.
*Row 7*: K1, p1, * k5/6, p7, k4, p2, k3, p1, k6/7, p2, **; rep from * to ** 3 times more, ending last rep with p1, k1, instead of p2.
*Row 8*: K2, * p4/5, p2 tog, k1, PFB, p2, k2, p4, yb, SSK, k3, k2 tog, p5/6, k2, **; rep from * to ** 3 times more.
*Row 9*: K1, p1, * k5/6, p5, k4, p2, k4, p1, k5/6, p2, **; rep from * to ** 3 times more, ending last rep with p1, k1, instead of p2.
*Row 10*: K2, * p5/6, M1k, k1, M1k, p4, k2, p4, yb, SSK, k1, k2 tog, p5/6, k2, **; rep from * to ** 3 times more.
*Row 11*: K1, p1, * k5/6, p3, k4, p2, k4, p3, k5/6, p2 **; rep from * to ** 3 times more, ending last rep with p1, k1, instead of p2.
*Row 12*: K2, * p5/6, (k1, M1k) twice, k1, p4, k1, M1k, k1, p2 tog, p2, yb, sl 2 knitwise, k1, p2sso, p5/6, k2, **; rep from * to ** 3 times more.
*Row 13*: K1, p1, * k9/10, p1, then p2, k4, p5, k5/6, p2, **; rep from * to ** 3 times more, ending last rep with p1, k1, instead of p2.
*Row 14*: K2, * p5/6, k2, M1k, k1, M1k, k2, p4, k1, KFB, k1, p2 tog, p7/8, k2, **; rep from * to ** 3 times more.
*Row 15*: K1, p1, * k8/9, p1, k1, p2, k4, p7, k5/6, p2, **; rep from * to ** 3 times more, ending last rep with p1, k1, instead of p2.
*Row 16*: K2, * p5/6, k3, M1k, k1, M1k, k3, p4, k2, PFB, k1, p2 tog, p6/7, k2, **; rep from * to ** 3 times more.
*Row 17*: K1, p1, * k7/8, p1, k2, p2, k4, p9, k5/6, p2, **; rep from * to ** 3 times more, ending last rep with p1, k1, instead of p2.
*Row 18*: K2, * p5/6, yb, SSK, k5, k2 tog, p4, k2, p1, PFB k1, p2 tog, p5/6, k2, **; rep from * to ** 3 times more.
*Row 19*: K1, p1, * k6/7, p1, k3, p2, k4, p7, k5/6, p2, **; rep from * to ** 3 times more, ending last rep with p1, k1, instead of p2.
*Row 20*: K2, * p5/6, yb, SSK, k3, k2

tog, p4, k2, p2, PFB, <u>k1,</u> p2 tog, p4/5, k2, **; rep from * to ** 3 times more.
*Row 21*: K1, p1, * k5/6, <u>p1,</u> k4, p2, k4, <u>p5,</u> k5/6, p2, **; rep from * to ** 3 times more, ending last rep with p1, k1 instead of p2.
*Row 22*: K2, * p5/6, yb, <u>SSK, k1, k2 tog,</u> p4, k2, p4, <u>M1k, k1, M1k,</u> p5/6, <u>k2 **</u>; rep from * to ** 3 times more.
*Row 23*: K1, p1, * k5/6, <u>p3,</u> k4, p2 k4, <u>p3,</u> K5/6, p2, **; rep from * to ** 3 times more, ending last rep with p1, k1, instead of p2.
*Row 24*: K2, * p5/6, yb, <u>sl 2 knit-wise, k1, p2sso,</u> p2, p2 tog, k1, <u>M1p</u> – see special abbreviations – k1, p4, <u>(k1, M1k) twice, k1,</u> p5/6, k2, **; rep from * to ** 3 times more.
These 24 rows form the patt.

With 3¼ mm ndls and MC cast on 98/106 sts. Work in k1, p1 rib for 5 cm (2 in).
*Inc row* (right side): Rib 1/8. * inc into next st. rib 5; rep from * 15/15 times more, then rib to end. 114/122 sts.
Change to 4 mm ndls.
Work the 24 rows of Leaf Patt three times and then row 1 of 4th patt – work should now measure about 33/33 cm (13/13 in) from cast-on edge.

**Shape armholes**
Cast off 3/3 sts at beg of next 2 rows, then dec 1 st at each end of next row and foll 2/2 alt rows. 102/110 sts. Work straight in patt until row 21 of 6th patt has been completed – work should now measure about 59.5/59.5 cm (23½/23½ in) from cast-on edge.
Cast off taking tog every 9th and 10th st.

With 3¼ mm ndls and MC cast on 52/54 sts.
Work in k1, p1, rib for 5 cm (2 in).
*Inc row*: Work in rib and inc 6/8 sts evenly across row. 58/62 sts.
Change to 4 mm ndls.
Work in patt following colours on diagram and rep from * to ** once instead of 3 times.
Row 1 will therefore read: k1, p1, * k5/6, p5, k4, p3, k9/10, p2, **; rep from * to ** once more, ending last rep with p1, k1 instead of p2.
Cont in patt as now set with col-oured leaves placed as indicated

on diagram until front measures same as back to armhole, ending at side edge.

**Shape armhole**
Cast off 3/3 sts at beg of next row, then dec 1 st at armhole edge of next row and foll 2/2 alt rows, 52/56 sts.
Work straight until row 10 of 6th patt has been completed – front should now measure about 56/56 cm (22/22 in) from cast-on edge.

**Shape neck**
Cast off 12/12 sts at beg (neck edge) of next row, then dec 1 st at neck edge of foll 7/8 rows. 33/36 sts.
Work straight until front measures same as back.
Cast off taking tog every 6th and 7th st.

Work as left front, reversing shap-ings and following colour sequ-ence for leaves as shown on diag-ram until row 9 of 6th patt has been completed.
Shape neck and finish as left front.

With 3¼ mm ndls and MC cast on 50/52 sts.
Work in k1, p1 rib for 5 cm (2 in).
*Inc row*: Work in rib and inc 12/12 sts evenly across row. 62/64 sts.
Change to 4 mm ndls.
Work in patt with rev. st st at each end and follow colour sequence for leaves as indicated on diagram.
*Row 1* (wrong side) will read thus: k1, p2, k next 13 sts (for rev. st st section), p2, then patt next 28/30 sts thus: k5/6, p5, k4, p3, k9/10, p2, k next 13 sts (for rev. st st), then p2, k1.
Work 9 rows as now set (i.e. work-ing centre panel in patt from * to ** once, with p2 before patt panel on wrong-side rows and k2 on right-side rows and keeping the sts within the 3 edge sts at each end in

rev. st st), then inc 1 st by working M1p within the 3 edge sts at each end of next row and every foll 6th row until there are 74/76 sts, working the extra sts in rev. st st as they occur, after which inc same way on every foll 4th row until there are 94/96 sts.

Cont straight until sleeve measures about 43/43 cm (17/17 in) from cast-on edge, ending with a wrong-side row.

**Shape top**

Cast off 3/3 sts at beg of next 2 rows, then dec 1 st at each end of next row and foll 15/16 alt rows, then dec 1 st at each end of every foll row until row 21 of 6th patt from beg has been completed.

Cast off rem sts.

## LEFT FRONT BAND

With 3¼ mm ndls and MC cast on 7 sts.

Work in k1, p1 rib until band, when slightly stretched, will fit up left front edge. Leave sts on a safety-pin.

Using a flat seam sew band neatly in position.

Mark positions for 7 buttons on band (8th one comes on neckband), the first 6 rows from bottom, the 7th, and 8th rows down from neck edge, the others evenly spaced between.

## RIGHT FRONT BAND

With 3¼ mm ndls and MC cast on 7 sts.

Work to match left front band, making buttonholes to match markers as follows:

*1st buttonhole row*: Rib 3, cast off 2, rib to end.

*2nd buttonhole row*: Work in rib, casting on 2 sts over those cast off to complete the buttonhole.

When 8th row after 7th buttonhole has been worked, leave sts on a safety-pin until required.

Using a flat seam sew band neatly in position.

## NECKBAND

Join shoulder seams, using a fine backstitch.

With 3¼ mm ndls and MC and right side of work facing rib across 7 sts left on safety-pin on right front band, pick up and k19/19 sts along right front neck edge to shoulder, 30/30 sts along back neck edge, 19/19 sts down left front neck edge, then rib the 7 sts from safety-pin on left front band. 82/82 sts.

Work 3 rows in rib, then work 8th buttonhole on the next 2 rows

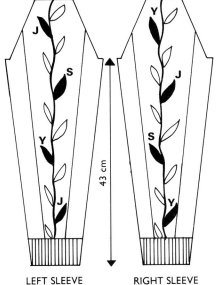

LEFT SLEEVE      RIGHT SLEEVE

43 cm

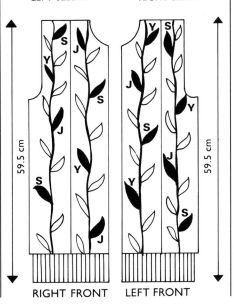

RIGHT FRONT    LEFT FRONT

59.5 cm

thus: rib 3, cast off 2, rib to end. On next row work in rib casting on 2 sts over those cast off.

Rib 2 rows more, then cast off in rib.

*To Make Up*

Do not press. Set sleeves into armholes, then join sleeve and side seams, using a fine backstitch. Sew 8 buttons to left front to correspond with the buttonholes. Sew in shoulder pads.

KEY TO COLOUR

**S**   SPANISH RED

**J**   JADE

**Y**   SUNFLOWER

BACK

59.5 cm

# Suit Yourself

ZIPPERED SWEATER WITH RIBBED SKIRT WHICH CAN BE KNITTED TO ANY LENGTH

## Stitches used

Two-and-two rib and stocking stitch.

## Sizes

Sweater – small/medium – to suit bust sizes 86/91 cm (34/36 in); length from shoulder 71 cm (28 in); sleeve 43 cm (17 in). Skirt – small/medium – hips 91–97 cm (36–38 in); length 45 cm (17½ in).

## Materials

Eleven/twelve 50g balls of Yarnworks Donegal Tweed Wool shade 904. Skirt six 50g balls of the same yarn. 30.5 cm (12 in) zip fastener; a length of elastic for skirt. The quantities of yarn specified are based on average requirements and are therefore approximate. If a longer skirt is required extra yarn will be needed.

## Needles

3 mm (no. 11), 4 mm (no. 8), 3¼ mm (no. 10), a set of four double-pointed (or circular) 3¾ mm (no. 9) for neckband; st-holders.

## Tension

Sweater: 20 sts and 28 rows to 10 cm (4 in) square measured over stocking stitch on 4 mm ndls. 38 sts and 32 rows over rib unstretched on 3¼ mm ndls.

## Note

Instructions given for two sizes for sweater, one size skirt.

# Instructions

## SWEATER
### BACK

** With 3 mm ndls cast on 102/106 sts.
*Row 1* (right side): K2, * p2, k2; rep from * to end.
*Row 2*: P2, * k2, p2; rep from * to end.
Rep last 2 rows for 20.5 cm (8 in), ending with a row 2.
Change to 4 mm ndls.
*Inc row*: P and inc 4/6 sts evenly across row. 106/112 sts. **
Cont straight in st st, beg with a k row, until back measures 71 cm (28 in) from cast-on edge. Cast off straight across.

### FRONT

Work as given for back from ** to ** 106/112 sts.
Now cont straight in st st, beg with a k row, until front measures 38 cm (15 in) from cast-on edge, ending with a p row.
Now introduce rib in centre as follows:
*Row 1* (right side): K52/55, p2, k52/55.
*Row 2*: P52/55, k2, p52/55.
Rep last 2 rows 4 times more.
*Row 11*: K49/52, p twice into next st, k2, p2, k2, p twice into next st, k49/52. 108/114 sts.
*Row 12*: P49/52, (k2, p2) twice, k2, p49/52.
*Row 13*: K49/52, (p2, k2) twice, p2, k49/52.
Rep last 2 rows 3 times more, then row 12 again.
*Row 21*: K46/49, p twice into next st, (k2, p2) 3 times, k2, p twice into next st, k46/49. 110/116 sts.
*Row 22*: P46/49, (k2, p2) 4 times, k2, p46/49.
Now divide for front opening thus:
*Row 23*: K46/49, (p2, k2) twice, turn; leaving rem 56/59 sts on a st-holder.
Cont on first set of 54/57 sts for left half front as follows:
*Row 24*: (P2, k2) twice, p46/49.
*Row 25*: K46/49, (p2, k2) twice.
Rep rows 24 and 25 twice more, then row 24 again.
*Row 31*: K43/46, p twice into next st, (p2, k2) twice, k2. 55/58sts.
*Row 32*: (P2, k2) 3 times, p43/46.
*Row 33*: K43/46, (p2, k2) 3 times.
Rep rows 32 and 33 three times more, then row 32 again.
*Row 41*: K40/43, p twice into next st, (k2, p2) 3 times, k2. 56/59 sts.
*Row 42*: (P2, k2) 4 times, p 40/43.
*Row 43*: K40/43, (p2, k2) 4 times.
Rep rows 42 and 43 three times more, then row 42 again.
*Row 51*: K37/40, p twice into next st, (k2, p2) 4 times, k2. 57/60 sts.
*Row 52*: (P2, k2) 5 times, p37/40.
*Row 53*: K37/40, (p2, k2) 5 times.
Rep rows 52 and 53 three times more, then row 52 again.
*Row 61*: K34/37, p twice into next st, (k2, p2) 5 times, k2. 58/61 sts.
*Row 62*: (P2, k2) 6 times, p34/37.
*Row 63*: K34/37, (p2, k2) 6 times.
Rep rows 62 and 63 three times more, then row 62 again.
*Row 71*: K31/34, p twice into next st, (k2, p2) 6 times, k2. 59/62 sts.
*Row 72*: (P2, k2) 7 times, p31/34.
*Row 73*: K31/34, (p2, k2) 7 times.
Rep rows 72 and 73 three times more, then row 72 again.
*Row 81*: K28/31, p twice into next st, (k2, p2) 7 times, k2, 60/63 sts.
*Row 82*: (P2, k2) 8 times, p28/31.
*Row 83*: K28/31, (p2, k2) 8 times.
Rep rows 82 and 83 twice more, then row 82 again.
*Row 89*: Cast off 26/29 sts loosely, then slip the st on right hand ndl on to left hand ndl and leave these rem 34 sts on a st-holder.
Rejoin yarn to rem 56/59 sts at centre front, cast off 2 purl sts (1st on ndl) k1, p2, k2, p2, then k to end. 54/57 sts.

### Right half front

Work to correspond with left half front from row 24 to row 88, but work all rows backwards, row 24 will read thus:
P46/49, (k2, p2) twice.
*Row 89* (right side): (K2, p2) 8 times, k28/31.
*Row 90*: Cast off 26/29 sts loosely for right shoulder, then slip the st on right hand ndl on to left-hand ndl and leave these rem 34 sts on a st-holder.

## RIBBED SHOULDERS

### Left shoulder

With two 3¾ mm ndls cast on 22 sts.
Work in k2, p2 rib (beg and ending

43

right side rows with p2) until piece fits along the 26/29 cast off sts of left front shoulder, ending with a wrong side row. (End with a right side row here on right shoulder.)
Now shape for back of neck as follows:
*Next row*: Rib 8, turn leaving the rem 14 sts on a spare ndl. Cont on these 8 sts and dec 1 st at inside edge on every row until all sts are worked off. Fasten off. Rejoin yarn to inside edge of rem 14 sts and rib across these 14 sts, then rib the 34 sts of left front from st-holder.
*Next row*: Rib across the 48/48 sts (omit this row on right shoulder). Leave these 48/48 sts on a spare ndl until required.

**Right shoulder**
Work this in the same way as left shoulder, but note items in brackets.

### RIBBED NECKBAND

Begin by pinning the row ends of shoulder ribbing to wrong side of the cast-off edges of respective shoulders on back and front and join with a fine backstitch, noting that the ribbed shoulders will extend across the back by the 8 rows of shaping – see diagram. Now with set of four 3¾ mm ndls (or circular ndl) and with right side of work facing begin at centre front opening of right front and rib 48 sts of right shoulder from spare ndl, pick up and k 8 sts from shaped edge of right shoulder, then pick up and k 30 sts across back neck edge, pick up and k 8 sts from shaped edge of left shoulder, after which rib the 48 sts from spare ndl of left front. 142/142 sts.
Rib one row across all these 142/142 sts.
Now shape as follows:
*Next 2 rows*: Rib to last 16 sts, turn; rib to last 16 sts, turn.
*Next 2 rows*: Rib to last 18 sts, turn; rib to last 18 sts, turn.
*Next 2 rows*: Rib to last 20 sts, turn;

rib to last 20 sts, turn.
*Next row*: Rib to end.
*Next row*: Rib across all sts.
Cont in rib until the front opening measures 31 cm (12¼ in). Cast off in rib, taking tog the 2 purl sts each time.

### SLEEVES (both alike)

With 3 mm ndls cast on 54/54 sts. Work 7.5 cm (3 in) in rib as given for back.
Change to 4 mm ndls.
Work 6 rows in st st, then inc 1 st at each end inside the first and last st on next row and every foll 3rd row, until there are 104/104 sts.
Work straight until sleeve measures 43 cm (17 in) from cast-on edge.
Cast off straight across.

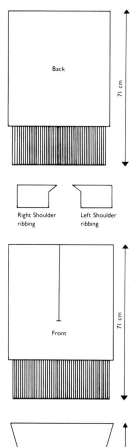

Do not press. Set in sleeves, placing centre of sleeve top to centre of ribbed shoulder. Join sleeve and side seams, using a fine backstitch. Insert zip fastener to front opening, using matching thread.

### SKIRT (back and front alike)

With 3¼ mm ndls cast on 170 sts. Work in k2, p2 rib, rows on right side having a k2 at each end until piece measures 39.5 cm (15½ in) from start ending with a row on

right side. Decrease for waist as follows:
*Dec row*: (wrong side facing) * p2 tog k2; rep from * to last 2 sts. P2 tog. (127 sts). Work 7.5 cm (3 in) straight in st st beg with a k row. Cast off loosely using a size larger needle.

Do not press. Join side seams with a flat seam on wrong side. Fold waist band in half to wrong side and hem in place, leaving a small opening. Insert elastic and close opening.

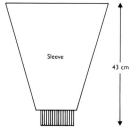

### Stitches used
Mainly in lattice stitch patt stocking stitch and moss stitch. One-and-one rib for welts, cuffs and collar.

### Sizes
Medium/large – to suit bust 89 to 94/96 to 101 cm (35 to 37/38 to 40 in); length from shoulder about 63.5 cm (25 in); sleeve about 43 cm (17 in).

### Materials
Eight/nine 50g balls of Yarnworks Donegal Tweed Wool shade 908 (MC) and one/one 50g ball of Yarnworks Merino Luxury Wool in each of the following contrast colours: Jade, Marigold, Spanish Red, Sunflower, shades 818, 821, 817, 820. The quantities of yarn specified are based on average requirements and are therefore approximate.

### Needles
$3\frac{1}{4}$ mm (no. 10), $4\frac{1}{2}$ mm (no. 7) and $3\frac{1}{4}$ mm (no. 10) circular needle for collar.

### Tension
22 sts and 24 rows to 10 cm (4 in) square measured over pattern on $4\frac{1}{2}$ mm ndls.

### Special abbreviations
Cr 2 R – cross 2 right (k into front of 2nd st from point of left hand needle, then k the first and slip both sts off needle tog); Cr 2 L – cross 2 left (k into back of the 2nd st from point of left hand needle, then k into first st and slip both sts off needle tog); MC – main colour; J – jade; M – marigold; S – sunflower; RE – Spanish red.

### Note
Instructions given for two sizes. The coloured diamonds are worked in moss stitch between the cross sts with the remainder of the diamonds in st st between cross sts. Do not strand MC across the back of the coloured diamonds – join in a 2nd ball of MC to work the

sts on the other side. Use separate lengths of yarn for each of the coloured diamonds, joining in and breaking off as required. Cross over yarns at back of work to avoid a hole. When working extra sts into moss stitch on the wrong side, always purl the new sts so that the MC does not show through on right side but gives a clear unbroken shape to the diamond.

**Working from chart**
One square represents one stitch and each square across, one row. Odd-numbered rows are read from right to left, even-numbered rows from left to right.

## Instructions

### LATTICE STITCH PATTERN

**Note**
On rows where coloured diamonds are worked, work the coloured diamond in m-st within the cross sts and the rest of the row in patt.
*Row 1* (right side): Cr 2 R (see special abbreviations), k12; rep from * to last 2 sts, Cr 2 R.
*Row 2 and alt rows*: P.
*Row 3*: K1, * Cr 2 L (see special abbreviations), k10, Cr 2 R; rep from * to last st, k1.
*Row 5*: * K2, Cr 2 L, k8, Cr 2 R; rep from * to last 2 sts, k2.
*Row 7*: K3, * Cr 2 L, k6, Cr 2 R, k4; rep from * ending last rep with k3, instead of k4.
*Row 9*: K4, * Cr 2 L, k4, Cr 2 R, k6; rep from * ending last rep with k4.
*Row 11*: K5, * Cr 2 L, k2, Cr 2 R, k8; rep from * ending last rep with k5.
*Row 13*: K6, * Cr 2 L, Cr 2 R, k10; rep from * ending last rep with k6.
*Row 15*: K7, * Cr 2 L, k12; rep from * ending last rep with k7.
*Row 17*: K6, * Cr 2 R, Cr 2 L, k10; rep from * ending last rep with k6.
*Row 19*: K5, * Cr 2 R, k2, Cr 2 L, k8; rep from * ending last rep with k5.
*Row 21*: K4, * Cr 2 R, k4, Cr 2 L, k6;

rep from * ending last rep with k4.
*Row 23*: K3, * Cr 2 R, k6, Cr 2 L, k4; rep from * ending last rep with k3.
*Row 25*: K2, * Cr 2 R, k8, Cr 2 L, k2; rep from * to end.
*Row 27*: K1, * Cr 2 R, k10, Cr 2 L; rep from * to last st, k1.
*Row 28*: P.
These 28 rows form lattice patt.

### BACK

With 3¼ mm ndls and MC cast on 110/118 sts.
Work in k1, p1 rib for 10 cm (4 in).
*Inc row*: (P26/10, inc into next st) 4/10 times, p2/8. 114/128 sts.
Change to 4½ mm ndls.
Cont in lattice patt and at same time introduce the coloured m-st diamonds as indicated on Chart A, working one diamond on rows 4, 18, 32, 46 and 60; 2 diamonds in M and S on row 74; one diamond on row 88; 2 diamonds in RE and J on row 102 and 2 diamonds in S and M on row 116.
Cont straight to the end of row 150 on Chart A. Back should now measure about 63.5 cm (25 in) from cast-on edge. Cast off straight across.

### FRONT

Work exactly as given for back until row 144 has been worked.

**Shape neck**
*Next row*: Patt 38/42, cast off 38/42. Cont on last set of 38/42 sts.
Work one row back to neck edge.
** Cast off 2 sts at beg (neck edge) on next row and foll alt row. Work one row straight, then cast off rem 34/38 sts.
Rejoin MC yarn to neck edge of rem 38/42 sts and work from ** on first side to end.

### SLEEVES (both alike)

With 3¼ mm ndls and MC cast on 52/56 sts.
Work in k1, p1 rib for 7.5 cm (3 in).
*Inc row*: Rib 6/4, (inc into next st, rib 1/2) 20/16 times, rib 6/4. 72/72 sts.
Change to 4½ mm ndls.
Work in lattice patt as for back, but follow Chart B for sleeve for positioning the m-st coloured diamonds and at same time inc 1 st at each end of 5th row and foll 6th row (as shown on Chart B for sleeve), after which inc 1 st at each end of every foll 4th row as indicated on Chart B. 112/112 sts.
Work straight to end row 90 of Chart B.
Sleeve should now measure about 43 cm (17 in), or work straight in lattice patt for required length.
Cast off straight across.

### COLLAR

Join shoulder seams, using a fine backstitch.
With 3¼ mm circular ndl, MC and right side of work facing begin at centre front, pick up and k 19/21 sts across 2nd half of cast-off edge at centre front, 6 sts up right neck edge, 50/54 sts across back of neck, 6 sts down left neck edge and 19/21 across first half of cast-off sts at centre front. 100/108 sts.
Work 3 rounds in k1, p1 rib.
Divide for front opening and work in rows as follows:
*Next row*: Rib 100/108 sts, turn.
*Next row*: Rib 100/108 sts, turn.
Cont in this way until collar measures 6.5 cm (2½ in).
Cast off in rib.

## To Make Up

Do not press. Set in sleeves, placing centre of cast-off sts to shoulder seam.
Join side and sleeve seams, using fine backstitch.

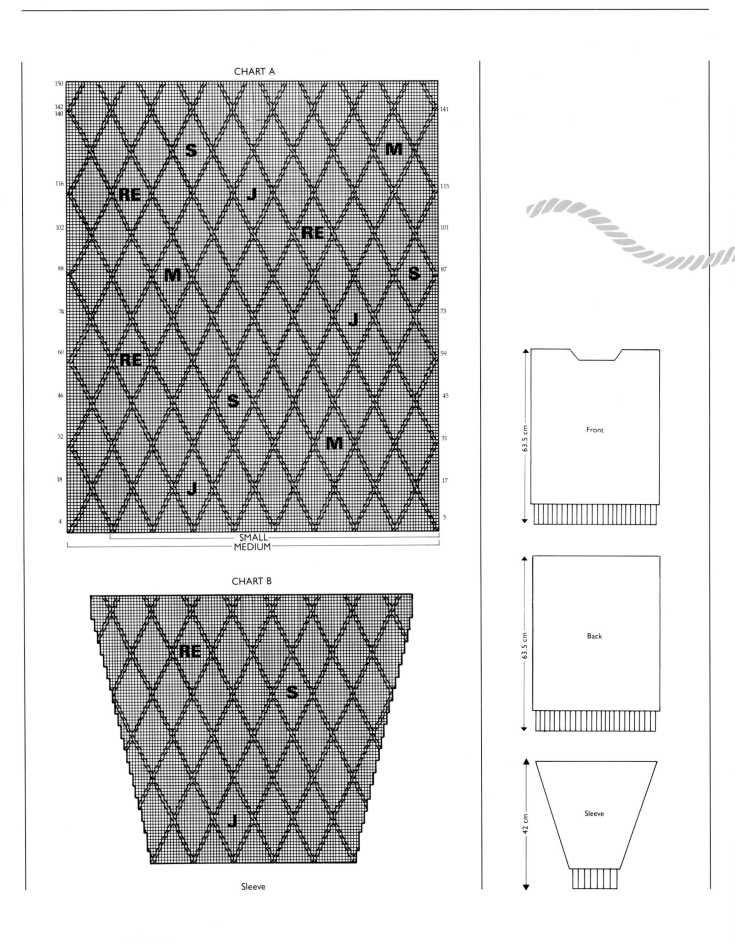

CHART A

SMALL
MEDIUM

CHART B

Sleeve

Front

Back

Sleeve

63.5 cm

63.5 cm

42 cm

# Brighton Belle

TRAVEL IN STYLE IN THIS WARM MOHAIR JACKET, WHICH HAS TWO SIDE POCKETS

**Stitches used**
Mainly in stocking stitch. Two-and-two rib for welts, cuffs, front bands and collar.

**Size**
Small/medium/large – to suit bust 86/91/96 cm (34/36/38 in); length 68.5 cm (27 in); sleeve seam 46 cm (18 in).

**Materials**
Seventeen/seventeen/eighteen 50g balls of Yarnworks French Poodle and one/one/one 50g ball of Yarn-works Merino Luxury Wool in a toning shade for pocket linings; six buttons; matching thread to join seams. The quantities of yarn specified are based on average requirements and are therefore approximate.

**Needles**
6 mm (no. 4); 10 mm (no. 000); 4½ mm (no. 7).

**Tension**
10 sts and 12 rows to 10 cm (4 in) square measured over stocking stitch on 10 mm ndls.

**Special abbreviations**
FP – French Poodle, O – No stitches to be worked in that size.

**Note**
Instructions given for three sizes.

## Instructions

### BACK

With 6 mm ndls and FP cast on 50/52/54 sts loosely.
Work in rib as follows:
*Row 1* (right side): P2/0/2, * k2, p2; rep from * to end.
*Row 2*: * k2, p2; rep from * to last 2/0/2 sts, k2/0/2.
Rep last 2 rows for 7.5 cm (3 in) from cast-on edge, ending with a row 2 and increasing 1 st at each end of last row. 52/54/56 sts.
Change to 10 mm ndls.

Cont in st st, beg with a k row, until back measures 40.5 cm (16 in) from cast-on edge, ending with a p row. Insert markers at each end of last row to denote beg of armholes. Cont straight until back measures 68.5 cm (27 in) from cast-on edge, ending with a p row.

**Shape shoulders**
Cast off 16/17/18 sts at beg of next 2 rows. Leave rem 20/20/20 sts on a spare ndl.

### LEFT FRONT

With 6 mm ndls and FP cast on 22/24/26 sts.
Work in rib as given for back for 7.5 cm (3 in), increasing 1 st at side seam of last row and ending with a row 2. 23/25/27 sts.
Change to 10 mm ndls.
Cont in st st until work measures 40.5 cm (16 in) from cast-on edge, ending with a p row. Insert marker at side seam edge on last row to denote beg of armhole.

**Shape front slope**
With right side of work facing, dec 1 st at front edge on next row and every foll 3rd row at front edge 7/8/9 times altogether. 16/17/18 sts. Work straight until work measures same as back to shoulder. Cast off straight across loosely.

### RIGHT FRONT

Work as left front, reversing all shaping.

### SLEEVES (both alike)

With 6 mm ndls and FP cast on 24/24/24 sts.
Work 6.5 cm (2½ in) in rib as given for back, following instructions given for medium size, ending with a row 2.
Change to 10 mm ndls.
Work 2 rows in st st, then inc 1 st at both ends of next row and every foll 4th row, until there are

46/46/46 sts.
Work straight until sleeve measures 46 cm (18 in) from cast-on edge. Cast off straight across loosely. Cast-off edge should measure 46 cm (18 in) across.

## RIBBED FRONT BANDS

### Left front bands
With 6 mm ndls and FP cast on 6 sts.
*Row 1* (right side): K2, p2, k2.
*Row 2*: P2, k2, p2.
Rep last 2 rows until band fits up left front, when slightly stretched, to beg of front slope shaping, ending with a row 2.
With right side facing inc 1 st at beg of next row and every foll alt row at shaped edge until there are 21/21/21 sts, working extra sts into rib as they are made, then inc 1 st at shaped edge on every foll 3rd row until there are 24/24/24 sts, still working extra sts into rib as they are made.

### Shape neck
*Next row* (right side): Rib 12, turn.
*Next row*: Rib back to shaped edge.
*Next 2 rows*: Rib 10, turn; rib back to shaped edge.
*Next 2 rows*: Rib 8, turn; rib back to shaped edge.
Leave sts on a spare ndl.
Sew band to left front, using matching thread and a flat seam.
Mark positions for 5 buttons on this band, the 1st one 1.3 cm (½ in) from lower edge, the 5th one just before turning rows on neck shaping, the others evenly spaced between.

### Right front band
Work as for left front band, reversing shaping and make 5 buttonholes to match markers (6th buttonhole comes in collar later), as follows:
*1st buttonhole row*: Rib 2, cast off 2, rib 1 more.
*2nd buttonhole row*: Work in rib, casting on 2 sts over those cast off to complete the buttonhole.
Begin the turning rows for neck shaping on a wrong side row to reverse the shaping.
When last row of shaping has been worked, rib across all sts thus finishing at front (straight) edge. Do not break off yarn.
Sew band in position.

## COLLAR

Using matching thread, join shoulder seams using a fine backstitch.
With 6 mm ndls rib along the 24 sts of right front band, then on to same ndl rib the 20 sts of back of neck from spare ndl, increasing 1 st at each end, then rib the 24 sts from spare ndl of left front band. (70 sts).
Work 15 cm (6 in) in rib, then work 6th buttonhole in next 2 rows. Rib one row more, then cast off in rib.

## POCKET LININGS

With 4½ mm ndls and FP cast on 18 sts.
Change to Merino and k one row, increasing 6 sts evenly across this row. (24 sts).
Cont in st st, beg with a p row, until work measures 14 cm (5½ in). Cast off.
Work 3 more pieces in the same way.
Join two pieces tog down two sides and across cast-off edge to make one pocket.

Do not press. Using matching thread sew cast-off edge of sleeve top between markers on back and fronts, using a fine backstitch. Join sleeve and side seams, leaving 12.5 cm (5 in) open above welts for pocket opening. Pin cast-on edge of pocket linings to open edge of back and fronts, just in from edge so that the Merino does not show, then with matching thread sew neatly in place. Catch-stitch loose ends of linings to fronts. Sew on buttons to correspond with buttonholes.

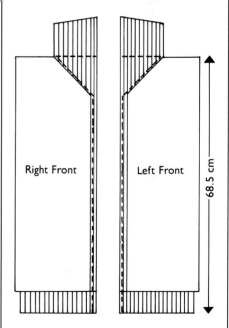

# Flying Scotsman

A SHAWL-COLLARED MOHAIR JACKET WITH ONE BUTTON AND TWO POCKETS

## Stitches used
Mainly in stocking stitch. Moss stitch for welts, front borders, cuffs and collar.

## Sizes
Small/medium/large – to suit bust sizes 86/91/97 cm (34/36/38 in); length from shoulder 51/54/56 cm (20/21¼/22 in); sleeve seam 38/40/42 cm (15/15¾/16½ in).

## Materials
Thirteen/fourteen/fourteen 50g balls of Yarnworks French Poodle; 1 large button; 2 shoulder pads; matching thread for making up. The quantities of yarn specified are based on average requirements and are therefore approximate.

## Needles
8 mm (no. 0); 10 mm (no. 000).

## Tension
9 sts and 12 rows to 10 cm (4 in) square measured over st st on 10 mm ndls.

## Note
Instructions given for three sizes.

## Instructions

### BACK

With 8 mm ndls cast on 41/45/47 sts.
Row 1: K1, (p1, k1) to end.
Rep this row 6 times more.
Change to 10 mm ndls.
Inc row: P to end inc 4 sts evenly across the row. 45/49/51 sts.
Beg with a k row, cont in st st until work measures 26 cm (10¼ in) from beg, ending with a p row.

#### Shape raglans
Next row: K1, skpo, k to last 3 sts, k2 tog, k1.
Next row: P to end.
Rep the last 2 rows until 15 sts rem, ending with a p row. Cast off.

### LEFT FRONT

With 8 mm ndls cast on 17/19/21 sts.
Row 1: K1, (p1, k1) to end.
Row 2: (K1, p1) into first st, (p1, k1) to end.
Row 3: (K1, p1) to last 2 sts, (k1, p1) into next st, k1.
Row 4: As row 1.
Row 5: K1, (p1, k1) to last 2 sts, (p1, k1) into next st, p1.
Row 6: (K1, p1) into first st, k1, (p1, k1) to end.
Row 7: As row 1.
Change to 10 mm ndls.
Row 8: (P1, k1 tbl) into first st, (p1, k1) twice, (p5, p into front and back of next st) twice, p to end.
Row 9: K to last 5 sts, p1, k1, p1, (k1, p1) into next st, k1. 25/27/29 sts.
Row 10: K1, (p1, k1) twice, p to end.
Row 11: K to last 4 sts, (p1, k1) twice.
Row 12: As row 10.
Rep the last 2 rows until work measures the same as back to armholes, ending with a wrong-side row.

#### Shape raglan and collar
Next row: K1, skpo, k to last 6 sts, m-st 6.
Next row: M-st 6, p to end.
Rep the last 2 rows twice more. 22/24/26 sts.
Next row: K1, skpo, k to last 7 sts m-st 7.
Next row: M-st 7, p to end.
Rep the last 2 rows twice more. 19/21/23 sts.
Next row: K1, skpo, k to last 8 sts, m-st 8.
Next row: M-st 8, p to end.
Rep the last 2 rows twice more. 16/18/20 sts.
Next row: K1, skpo, k to last 9 sts, m-st 9.
Next row: M-st 9, p to end.
Rep the last 2 rows twice more. (13/15/17 sts).
Next row: K1, skpo, k0/2/4, m-st 10. (12/14/16 sts).
Next row: M-st 10, p to end.
Next row: K1, skpo, k0/1/3, m-st 9/10/10. (11/13/15 sts).
Next row: M-st 10, p to end.
Next row: K1, skpo, k0/0/2, m-st 8/10/10. (10/12/14 sts).
Next row: M-st 10, p0/2/4.
Next row: (K1, skpo) 0/1/1 time, m-st 10/9/11. (10/11/13 sts).
Next row: M-st 10, p0/1/2.
Next row: (K1, skpo) 0/1/1 time, m-st 10/8/10. (10/10/12 sts).
Next row: M-st 10, p0/0/2.
Next row: (K1, skpo) 0/0/1 time, m-st 10/10/9. 10/10/11 sts.
Next row: M-st 10/10/11.
Next row: (K1, skpo) 0/0/1 time, m-st 10/10/8. 10/10/10 sts.
Cont in m-st on rem 10 sts until work measures 19 cm (7½ in) from last dec.
Cast off.

### SLEEVES

With 8 mm ndls cast on 21 sts.
Row 1: K1, (p1, k1) to end.
Rep this row 6 times more.
Change to 10 mm ndls.
Beg with a p row, cont in st st, inc one st at each end of the 3rd and every foll 4th row until there are 39/41/43 sts.
Cont without shaping until work measures 38/40/42 cm (15/15¾/16½ in) from beg, ending with a p row.

#### Shape top
Next row: K1, skpo, k to last 3 sts, k2 tog, k1.
Next row: P to end.
Rep the last 2 rows until 31/33/33 sts rem, ending with a p row.
** Work 2 rows straight.
Next row: K1, skpo, k to last 3 sts, k2 tog, k1.
Next row: P to end. **
Rep from ** to ** 1(2/2) times more. 27 sts.
Work 2 rows straight.
Next row: K1, skpo, k8, skpo, k1, k2 tog, k8, k2 tog, k1. 23 sts.
Next row: P to end.
Next row: K1, skpo, k to last 3 sts, k2 tog, k1. 21 sts.
Next row: P to end.
Next row: K1, skpo, k5, skpo, k1,

k2 tog, k5, k2 tog, k1. 17 sts.
*Next row*: P to end.
*Next row*: K1, skpo, k to last 3 sts,
k2 tog, k1. 15 sts.
*Next row*: P to end.
*Next row*: K1, skpo, k2, skpo, k1,
k2 tog, k2, k2 tog, k1. 11 sts.
*Next row*: P to end.
*Next row*: K1, skpo, k to last 3 sts,
k2 tog, k1. 9 sts.
*Next row*: P to end.
Cast off.

## RIGHT FRONT

With 8 mm ndls cast on 17/19/21
sts.
*Row 1*: K1, (p1, k1) to end.
*Row 2*: K1, (p1, k1) to last 2 sts, (p1,
k1 tbl) into next st, k1.
*Row 3*: (K1, p1) into first st, k1, (p1,
k1) to end.
*Row 4*: As row 1.
*Row 5*: (P1, k1 tbl) into first st, (p1,
k1) to end.
*Row 6*: K1, (p1, k1) to last 3 sts, p1,
(k1, p1) into next st, k1. (21/23/25
sts).
*Row 7*: As row 1.
Change to 10 mm ndls.
*Row 8*: (P5, p into front and back of
next st) twice, p to last 7 sts, (k1,
p1) twice, k1, (p1, k1 tbl) into next
st, k1.
*Row 9*: (K1, p1) into first st, k1 (p1,
k1) twice, k to end. 25/27/29 sts.
*Row 10*: P to last 5 sts, k1, (p1, k1)
twice.
*Row 11*: (K1, p1) twice, k to end.
*Row 12*: As row 10.
Rep the last 2 rows once more.

### Work buttonhole
*Row 15*: M-st 3, turn, m-st 3, turn,
m-st 3, break off yarn, rejoin to rem
22/24/26 sts, p1, k to end.
*Row 16*: P to last 5 sts, k1, p1, turn.
*Row 17*: P1, k to end.
*Row 18*: As row 10. 25/27/29 sts.
Rep rows 10 and 11 until work
measures the same as back to
armholes, ending with a wrong-
side row.

### Shape raglan and collar
*Next row*: (K1, p1) 3 times, k to last

3 sts, k2 tog, k1.
*Next row*: P to last 6 sts, m-st 6.
Rep the last 2 rows twice more.
22/24/26 sts.
*Next row*: (K1, p1) 3 times, k to last
3 sts, k2 tog, k1.
*Next row*: P to last 7 sts, m-st 7.
Rep the last 2 rows twice more.
19/21/23 sts.
*Next row*: (K1, p1) 4 times, k to last
3 sts, k2 tog, k1.
*Next row*: P to last 8 sts, m-st 8.
Rep the last 2 rows twice more.
16/18/20 sts.
*Next row*: (K1, p1) 4 times, k to last
3 sts, k2 tog, k1.
*Next row*: P to last 9 sts, m-st 9.
Rep the last 2 rows twice more.
13/15/17 sts.
*Next row*: (K1, p1) 5 times, k0/2/3,
k2 tog, k1. 12/14/16 sts.
*Next row*: P to last 10 sts, m-st 10.
*Next row*: (K1, p1) 4/5/5 times, k to
last 3 sts, k2 tog. 11/13/15 sts.
*Next row*: P1/3/5, m-st 10.
*Next row*: (K1, p1) 4/5/5 times,
k0/0/2, k2 tog, k1. 10/12/14 sts.
*Next row*: P0/2/4, m-st 10.
*Next row*: (K1, p1) 5/4/5 times,
k0/1/1, (k2 tog, k1) 0/1/1 time.
10/11/13 sts.
*Next row*: P0/1/3, m-st 10.
*Next row*: (K1, p1) 5/4/4 times,
k0/0/2, (k2 tog, k1) 0/1/1 time.
10/10/12 sts.
*Next row*: P0/0/2, m-st 10.
*Next row*: (K1, p1) 5/5/4 times, (k2
tog, k1) 0/0/1 time. 10/10/11 sts.
*Next row*: M-st 10/10/11.
*Next row*: (K1, p1) 5/5/4 times, (k2
tog, k1) 0/0/1 time. 10/10/10 sts.
Cont in m-st on rem 10 sts until
work measures 19 cm (7½ in) from
last dec.
Cast off.

## To Make Up

Do not press. Join raglan seams.
Join side and sleeve seams with
matching thread, using a fine
backstitch. Join cast-off edges of

collar with a flat seam, and sew in
place along sleeve tops and back
neck. Sew in shoulder pads. Sew
on button.

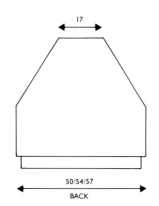

17

50/54/57
BACK

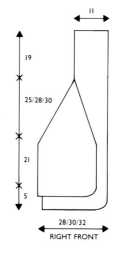

11

19

25/28/30

21

5

28/30/32
RIGHT FRONT

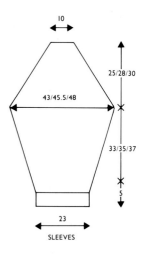

10

25/28/30

43/45.5/48

33/35/37

5

23
SLEEVES

# Candy Floss

## Stitches used

Mainly in panels of cable and lace. Welts, cuffs and neck border in two-and-two rib.

## Sizes

Small/medium/large – to suit bust 86/91/97 cm (34/36/38 in); length 64/66/66 cm (25/26/26 in); sleeve seam 46 cm (18 in).

## Materials

Twenty-one / twenty-two / twenty-two 25g balls of Yarnworks Shaggy Dog or Shaggy Dog Sparkle.
The quantities of yarn specified are based on average requirements and are therefore approximate.

## Needles

5 mm (no. 6); 7 mm (no. 2); cable needle.

## Tension

14 sts and 16 rows to 10 cm (4 in) square measured over reverse stocking stitch on 7 mm needles.

## Note

Instructions given for three sizes.

## Special abbreviations

C8F – Cable 8 front, sl next 4 sts on to cable ndl and leave at front of work, k4 then k4 from cable ndl; C8B – Cable 8 back, sl next 4 sts on to cable ndl and leave at back of work, k4 than k4 from cable ndl; C4F – Cable 4 front, sl next 2 sts on to cable ndl and leave at front of work, k2 then k2 from cable ndl.

# Instructions

## BACK AND FRONT (alike)

With 5 mm ndls cast on 68/72/76 sts.
Work 7.5 cm (3 in) in k2, p2 rib.
Inc row: Rib 6/3/5, * inc in next st, rib 4/5/5; rep from * to last 7/3/5 sts, inc in next st, rib to end. 80/84/88 sts.

## NECK BORDER

Change to 7 mm ndls and work in patt as follows:
Row 1 (right side): P2/4/6, * k2, yf, k2 tog, p4, k3, yf, k2 tog, k4, yf, k2 tog, k1, p4, k2, yf, k2 tog *, p4, k12, p4; rep from * to * once more, p2/4/6.
Row 2: K2/4/6, * p2, yrn, p2 tog, k4, p3, yrn, p2 tog, p4, yrn, p2 tog, p1, k4, p2, yrn, p2 tog *, k4, p12, k4; rep from * to * once more, k2/4/6.
Rows 3 and 4: As rows 1 and 2.
Row 5: P2/4/6, * C4F, p4, k3, yf, k2 tog, k4, yf, k2 tog, k1, p4, C4F *, p4, k4, C8B, p4; rep from * to * once more, p2/4/6.
Row 6: As row 2.
Rows 7 to 10: As rows 1 to 4.
Row 11: P2/4/6, * k2, yf, k2 tog, p4, k3, yf, k2 tog, k4, yf, k2 tog, k1, p4, k2, yf, k2 tog *; p4, C8F, k4, p4; rep from * to * once more, p2/4/6.
Row 12: As row 2.

*Rows 13 to 18*: As rows 1 to 6.
*Rows 19 and 20*: As rows 1 and 2.
*Row 21*: P2/4/6, * k2, yf, k2 tog, p4, k12, p4, rep from * twice more, k2, yf, k2 tog, p2/4/6.
*Row 22*: K2/4/6, * p2, yrn, p2 tog, k4, p12, k4; rep from * twice more, p2, yrn, p2 tog, k2/4/6.
*Row 23*: P2/4/6, * k2, yf, k2 tog, p4, C8F, k4, p4; rep from * twice more, k2, yf, k2 tog, p2/4/6.
*Row 24*: As row 22.
*Row 25*: P2/4/6, * k2, yf, k2 tog, p4, k12, p4, k2, yf, k2 tog *; p4, k3, yf, k2 tog, k4, yf, k2 tog, k1, p4; rep from * to * once more, p2/4/6.
*Row 26*: K2/4/6, * p2, yrn, p2 tog, k4, p12, k4, p2, yrn, p2 tog *; k4, p3, yrn, p2 tog, p4, yrn, p2 tog, p1, k4; rep from * to * once more, k2/4/6.
*Rows 27 and 28*: As rows 25 and 26.
*Row 29*: P2/4/6, * C4F, p4, k4, C8B, p4, C4F *; p4, k3, yf, k2 tog, k4, yf, k2 tog, k1, p4; rep from * to * once more, p2/4/6.
*Row 30*: As row 26.
*Rows 31 to 34*: As rows 25 to 28.
*Row 35*: P2/4/6, * k2, yf, k2 tog, p4, C8F, k4, p4, k2, yf, k2 tog *; p4, k3, yf, k2 tog, k4, yf, k2 tog, k1, p4; rep from * to * once more, p2/4/6.
*Row 36*: As row 26.
*Rows 37 to 42*: As rows 25 to 30.
*Rows 43 and 44*: As rows 25 and 26.
*Rows 45 to 48*: As rows 21 to 24.
These 48 rows form the patt.
Rep them until work measures 40/41/41 cm (15¾/16/16 in) from cast-on edge. Mark each end of last row. Cont straight until work measures 59/60/60 cm (23/23½/23½ in) from cast-on edge, ending with a wrong side row and inc 1 st at each end of last row. 82/86/90 sts.

## NECK BORDER

Change to 5 mm ndls and work in rib for neck border as follows:
*Row 1*: K2, * p2, k2; rep from * to end.

*Row 2*: P2, * k2, p2; rep from * to end.
Rep these 2 rows until rib measures 5/6/6 cm (2/2½/2½ in) ending with a row 2. Cast off in rib.

## LEFT SLEEVE

With 5 mm ndls cast on 38 sts.
Work 6 cm (2½ in) in rib as given for neck border, ending with row 1.
*Inc row*: Rib 6, * inc in next st, rib 7; rep from * to end. 42 sts.
Change to 7 mm ndls and work in patt as follows: **
*Row 1 (right side)*: P3, k3, yf, k2 tog, k4, yf, k2 tog, k1, p4, k2, yf, k2 tog, p4, k12, p3.
*Row 2*: K3, p12, k4, p2, yrn, p2 tog, k4, p3, yrn, p2 tog, p4, yrn, p2 tog, p1, k3.
*Row 3*: P1, inc in next st, p1, k3, yf, k2 tog, k4, yf, k2 tog, k1, p4, k2, yf, k2 tog, p4, k12, p1, inc in next st, p1.
*Row 4*: K4, p12, k4, p2, yrn, p2 tog, k4, p3, yrn, p2 tog, p4, yrn, p2 tog, p1, k4.
*Row 5*: P4, k3, yf, k2 tog, k4, yf, k2 tog, k1, p4, C4F, p4, k4, C8B, p4.
*Row 6*: As row 4.
These 6 rows establish position of the patt. Cont in patt as set, inc 1 st inside first and last st on next row and every foll 4th row until there are 72 sts, working the next 4 inc sts at each end into small lace panel and the remainder of the inc sts into reverse st st.
Work straight until sleeve measures 46 cm (18 in) from cast-on edge, ending with a wrong side row. Cast off loosely.

## RIGHT SLEEVE

Work as for left sleeve to **.
*Row 1 (right side)*: P3, k12, p4, k2, yf, k2 tog, p4, k3, yf, k2 tog, k4, yf, k2 tog, k1, p3.
*Row 2*: K3, p3, yrn, p2 tog, p4, yrn, p2 tog, p1, k4, p2, yrn, p2 tog, k4, p12, k3.
*Row 3*: P1, inc in next st, p1, k12,

p4, k2, yf, k2 tog, p4, k3, yf, k2 tog, k4, yf, k2 tog, k1, p1, inc in next st, p1.
*Row 4*: K4, p3, yrn, p2 tog, p4, yrn, p2 tog, p1, k4 p2, yrn, p2 tog, k4, p12, k4.
*Row 5*: P4, k4, C8B, p4, C4F, p4, k3, yf, k2 tog, k4, yf, k2 tog, k1, p4.
*Row 6*: As row 4.
Complete as given for left sleeve.

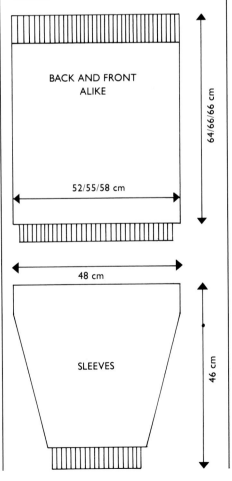

## To Make Up

Join shoulder seams with plain matching yarn, leaving 28 cm (11 in) open at centre for neck. Set in sleeves between markers. Join side and sleeve seams using a fine back stitch.

BACK AND FRONT ALIKE

64/66/66 cm

52/55/58 cm

48 cm

SLEEVES

46 cm

# Sea Cruise

**Stitches used**
Mainly in stocking stitch. Two-and-two rib for welts, cuffs and neckband.

**Sizes**
Small/medium/large – to suit bust 86/91/97 cm (34/36/38 in); length 68.5 cm (27 in); sleeve seam 52 cm (20½ ins).

**Materials**
Ten/eleven/eleven 50g balls of Yarnworks Merino Sport in main colour and three/three/three 50g balls of the same yarn in contrast.

**Needles**
4½ mm (no. 7); 5½ mm (no. 5); stitch-holder.

**Tension**
17 sts and 21 rows to 10 cm (4 in) square measured over stocking stitch on 5½ mm ndls.

## Instructions

### BACK

With 4½ mm ndls and MC cast on 92/96/100 sts. Work in k2, p2, rib for 7.5 cm (3 in).
Change to 5½ mm ndls.
Work in stripe patt as follows:
*Row 1* (right side): With C, k.
*Row 2*: With C, p.
*Row 3*: With MC, k.
*Row 4*: With MC, p.
*Rows 5 and 6*: As rows 3 and 4.
*Row 7*: As row 3.
*Row 8*: With C, p.
*Row 9*: With C, k.
*Row 10*: With MC, p.
*Row 11*: With MC, k.
*Rows 12 and 13*: As rows 10 and 11.
*Row 14*: As row 10.
These 14 rows form stripe patt. Rep them until back measures 43 cm (17 in) from cast-on edge, ending with a p row.

**Shape armholes**
Cast off 9 sts at beg of next 2 rows. 74/78/82 sts.
Still working in stripe patt cont straight until back measures 68.5 cm (27 in) from cast-on edge, ending with a p row.

**Shape shoulders**
Cast off 13/14/15 sts at beg of next 2 rows, then cast off 12/13/14 sts at beg of foll 2 rows. Leave rem 24/24/24 sts on a spare ndl.

### FRONT

Work as given for back until armhole shaping has been worked. 74/78/82 sts.
Now cont as follows:
Work straight in stripe patt until front measures 53.5 cm (21 in) from cast-on edge, ending with a p row.
Divide for front opening thus:
*Next row* (right side): K31/33/35 sts and leave these sts on a st-holder for left half front, cast off next 12 sts, then k to end of row. 31/33/35 sts.

### RIGHT HALF FRONT

Cont in stripe patt on these 31/33/35 sts until work measures 62 cm (24½ in) from cast-on edge, ending at neck edge.

**Shape neck**
** Dec 1 st at neck edge on next row and every foll alt row until 25/27/29 sts rem.
Cont straight until work measures same as back to shoulder, ending at armhole edge.

**Shape shoulder**
Cast off 13/14/15 sts at beg of next row. Work one row straight, then cast off.
Return to the rem 31/33/35 sts left on a st-holder and rejoin yarn at neck edge and work from ** on right half front to end.

### SLEEVES (both alike)

With 4½ mm ndls and MC cast on 40/44/44 sts. Work 6.5 cm (2½ in) in k2, p2 rib, increasing 1 st at end of last row. 41/45/45 sts.
Change to 5½ mm ndls.
Work 2 rows in stripe patt as given for back, then still working in stripe patt inc 1 st at each end of next row and every foll 3rd row, until there are 93/97/97 sts.
Work straight until sleeve measures 52 cm (20½ in) from cast-on edge, ending with a p row. Cast off.

### LEFT FRONT BAND

With right side of work facing, 4½ mm ndls and MC pick up and k 18 sts along row ends of left front opening.
Work in k2, p2 rib for 6.5 cm (2½ in), beg and ending right side rows with k2. Cast off in rib.

### RIGHT FRONT BAND

Work right front band in the same way as left front band.

### NECKBAND

Join shoulder seams, using a fine backstitch.
With 4½ mm ndls, MC and the right side of work facing beg at centre of right front band and pick up and k 8 sts, then pick up and k 21 sts along neck edge of right half front, k 24 sts from spare ndl at back neck, after which pick up and k 21 sts down neck edge of left half front and 8 sts along left front band, ending at centre of band. 82/82/82 sts.
Work 6.5 cm (2½ in) in k2, p2 rib beg and ending wrong side rows with p2 and right side rows with k2. Cast off in rib.

59

## To Make Up

Do not press. Measure 5 cm (2 in) down from cast-off edge of sleeve top and mark with pins. Set in sleeves, placing the row ends above pins to cast-off sts at armholes. Join sleeve and side seams, using a fine backstitch. Sew row ends at base of left front band in place and base of right front band on top of it.

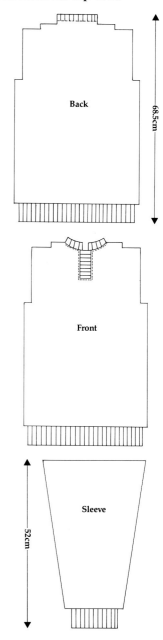

# Deckhand

## Stitches used
Mainly panels of cable on reverse stocking stitch. Welts, cuffs and neckband in one-and-one rib.

## Sizes
To fit chest sizes 91/97 102/107 112/117 cm (36/38 40/42 44/46 in); full length 64/65/66 cm (25/25½/26 in); sleeve length 48/48/48 cm (19/19/19 in).

## Materials
Eighteen/nineteen/twenty 50g balls of Yarnworks Merino Sport.

## Needles
4½ mm (no. 7); 5½ mm (no. 5). Cable needle.

## Tension
17 sts and 21 rows to 10 cm (4 in) measured over stocking stitch on 5½ mm ndls.

## Special abbreviations
C9 – cable 9 (sl next 4 sts on to a cable ndl and leave at back of work, k next 5 sts then k4 from cable ndl); M1 – make 1 by picking up thread between st just worked and next st and p into back of it.

# Instructions

### BACK

With 4½ mm ndls cast on 81/91/101 sts.
*Row 1* (right side): K1, * p1, k1, rep from * to end.
*Row 2*: P1, * k1, p1, rep from * to end.
These 2 rows form rib.
Cont until work measures 6 cm (2½ in) from beg, ending with row 1.
*Inc row*: Rib 3/8/13, M1, * rib 4, M1, rep from * to last 2/7/12 sts, rib to end. 101/111/121 sts.
Change to 5½ mm ndls and patt.
*Row 1* (right side): P5, * k1 tbl, p4/5/6, k9, p4/5/6, rep from * to last 6 sts, k1 tbl, p5.
*Row 2 and every alt row*: K5, * p1 tbl, k4/5/6, p9, k4/5/6, rep from * to last 6 sts, p1 tbl, k5.
*Row 3*: As row 1.
*Row 5*: P5, * k1 tbl, p4/5/6, C9, p4/5/6, rep from * to last 6 sts, k1 tbl, p5.
*Row 7*: As row 1.
*Row 9*: As row 1.
*Row 11*: As row 1.
*Row 12*: As row 2.
These 12 rows form patt.
Cont in patt until work measures 38/37/36 cm (15/14½/14 in) from beg, ending with a wrong side row.
Cast off.

## FRONT

Work as back.

## SLEEVES AND YOKE

Worked in one piece beg with left sleeve.

With 4½ mm ndls cast on 41/45/49 sts and work 9 cm (3½ in) in rib as given for back, ending with row 1.
*Inc row*: P5/4/3, M1, * p1, M1, rep from * to last 5/4/3 sts, p to end. 73/83/93 sts.
Change to 5½ mm ndls and patt.
*Row 1 (right side)*: P2, * k9, p1/2/3, k1 tbl, p1/2/3; rep from * to last 11 sts, k9, p2.
*Row 2 and every alt row*: K2, * p9, k1/2/3, p1 tbl, k1/2/3; rep from * to last 11 sts, p9, k2.
*Row 3*: As row 1.
*Row 5*: P2, * C9, p1/2/3, k1 tbl, p1/2/3; rep from * to last 11 sts, C9, p2.
*Row 7*: As row 1.
*Row 9*: As row 1.
*Row 11*: As row 1.
*Row 12*: As row 2.
These 12 rows set the patt.
Work 12 more rows in patt.
*Next row*: P2, * k9, p1/2/3, M1, k1 tbl, M1, p1/2/3; rep from * to last 11 sts, k9, p2. 83/93/103 sts.
*Next row*: K2, * p9, k2/3/4, p1 tbl, k2/3/4; rep from * to last 11 sts, p9, k2.
Keeping patt correct work 22 rows more in patt as set.
*Next row*: P2, * k9, p2/3/4, M1, k1 tbl, M1, p2/3/4; rep from * to last 11 sts, k9, p2. 93/103/113 sts.
*Next row*: K2, * p9, k3/4/5, p1 tbl, k3/4/5; rep from * to last 11 sts, p9, k2.
Keeping patt correct work 22 rows more in patt as set.
*Next row*: P2, * k9, p3/4/5, M1, k1 tbl, M1, p3/4/5; rep from * to last 11 sts, k9, p2. 103/113/123 sts.
*Next row*: K2, * p9, k4/5/6, p1 tbl,

k4/5/6, rep from * to last 11 sts. p9, k2.
Keeping patt correct work 14 rows in patt as set.
Place a coloured marker at each end of last row.
Work 30/36/42 rows straight in patt.

**Shape neck**
*Next row*: Patt 51/56/61, cast off next 5/7/9 sts, patt to end.
*Next row*: Patt 47/50/53, turn. Leave rem sts on a spare ndl.
Keeping patt correct, cast off 2 sts at beg of next row and every foll alt row 6 times more. 33/36/39 sts.
Work 21 rows straight.
Cast on 2 sts at beg of next row and every foll alt row 6 times more. 47/50/53 sts. Work 1 row straight.
Break off yarn, leaving these sts on a spare ndl.
With wrong side facing, rejoin yarn to 51/56/61 sts left on spare ndl and patt to end.
Work 6 rows dec 1 st at end of next row and foll 4th row. 49/54/59 sts.
Work 36 rows straight.
Work 6 rows inc 1 st at end of next row and foll 4th row. 51/56/61 sts.
*Next row*: Patt to end, cast on 5/7/9 sts, then patt across 47/50/53 sts left on spare ndl. 103/113/123 sts.
Work 31/37/43 rows straight in patt.
Place a coloured marker at each end of last row.
Work 14 rows straight.
*Next row*: P2, * k9, p2/3/4, p2 tog, k1 tbl, p2 tog, p2/3/4; rep from * to last 11 sts, k9, p2.
*Next row*: K2, * p9, k3/4/5, p1 tbl, k3/4/5; rep from * to last 11 sts, p9, k2. 93/103/113 sts.
Work 22 rows more in patt as set.
*Next row*: P2, * k9, p1/2/3, p2 tog, k1 tbl, p2 tog, p1/2/3; rep from * to last 11 sts, k9, p2. 83/93/103 sts.
*Next row*: K2, * p9, k2/3/4, p1 tbl, k2/3/4; rep from * to last 11 sts, p9, k2.
Work 22 rows more in patt as set.
*Next row*: P2, * k9, p0/1/2, p2 tog, k1 tbl, p2 tog, p0/1/2; rep from * to last 11 sts, k9, p2. 73/83/93 sts.
*Next row*: K2, * p9, k1/2/3, p1 tbl,

k1/2/3; rep from * to last 11 sts, p9, k2.
Work 22 rows more in patt as set.
Change to 4½ mm ndls.
*Dec row*: K4/3/2, (k2 tog) 32/38/44 times, k5/4/3. 41/45/49 sts.
Beg with row 2 work 9 cm (3½ in) in rib as given for back, ending with row 2.
Cast off in rib.

## BACK NECKBAND

With right side facing and 4½ mm ndls, pick up and k40 sts evenly from back neck.
Beg with row 2 work 2½ cm (1 in) in rib as given for back, ending with row 2.
Cast off in rib.

## FRONT NECKBAND

With right side facing and 4½ mm ndls, pick up and k56/60/64 sts evenly along front neck.
Beg with row 2 work 2½ cm (1 in) in rib as given for back, ending with row 2.
Cast off in rib.

*To Make Up*

Sew side edges of neckband together. Sew cast off edges of back and front between markers. Sew side and sleeve seams.

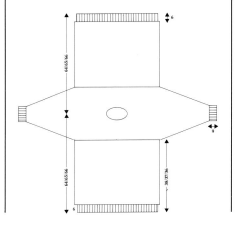

# First Mate

THIS TUNIC-STYLE SWEATER HAS AN ORIGINAL NECK OPENING

## Stitches used

Mainly in stocking stitch. Two-and-two rib for welts, cuffs and inset.

## Sizes

Small/medium/large – to suit bust 86/91/97 cm (34/36/38 in); length 66/68/70 cm (26/26¾/27 ins); sleeve seam 46 cm (16½ in).

## Materials

Thirteen/fourteen/fifteen 50g balls of Yarnworks Merino Sport; 6 small buttons.

## Needles

4½ mm (no. 7); 5 mm (no. 6); 5½ mm (no. 5); stitch-holder.

## Tension

17 sts and 21 rows to 10 cm (4 in) square measured over stocking stitch on 5½ mm ndls.

## Instructions

### BACK

With 5½ mm ndls cast on 120/128/136 sts. Work in rib as follows:
*Row 1* (right side): K3, * p2, k2; rep from * to last 5 sts, p2, k3.
*Row 2*: P3, * k2, p2; rep from * to last 5 sts, k2, p3.
Rep last 2 rows until work measures 7.5 cm (3 in) from cast-on edge, ending with row 1.
*Next row* (wrong side): P3, (k2, p2) 4 times, then * k2 tog, p2; rep from * to last 17 sts, (k2, p2) 4 times, then p1. 99/105/111 sts.
Cont as follows:
*Row 1* (right side): K3, (p2, k2) 4 times, k to last 17 sts, (p2, k2) 4 times, then k1.
*Row 2*: P3, (k2, p2) 4 times, then p to last 17 sts, (k2, p2) 4 times, then p1.

Rep last 2 rows until back measures 15 cm (6 in) from cast-on edge, ending with row 1.
*Next row* (wrong side): P3, (k2 tog, p2) 4 times, then p to last 17 sts (k2 tog, p2) 4 times, then p1. 91/97/103 sts.
Cont entirely in st st, beg with a k row, until back measures 39.5 cm (15½ in) from cast-on edge, ending with a p row. ***

### Shape raglan

Cast off 4 sts at beg of next 2 rows.
*Row 3*: K2, skpo, k to last 4 sts, k2 tog, k2.
*Row 4*: P.
Rep rows 3 and 4 until 33/35/37 sts rem, ending with a row 4, then dec 1 st at each end of every foll row as follows:
*Next row*: As row 3.
*Next row*: P2, p2 tog tbl, p to last 4 sts, p2 tog, p2.
Rep last 2 rows until 25/27/29 sts rem. Leave these sts on a spare ndl.

### FRONT

Work as back to ***, then cont as follows:
Shape raglan and divide for neck thus:
*Row 1*: Cast off 4 sts, (1 st on ndl), k39/42/45 sts, skpo, turn; leaving the rem 45/48/51 sts on a spare ndl.

### LEFT HALF FRONT

Cont on first set of 41/44/47 sts thus:
*Row 1*: P.
*Row 2*: K2, skpo, k to end.
*Row 3*: P.
Dec 1 st at armhole edge on next row and every foll alt row, at the same time dec 1 st at neck edge on next row and every foll 4th row until 4 sts rem.
*Next row*: P.
*Next row*: K2, skpo.
*Next row*: P.
*Next row*: K1, skpo.
*Next row*: P2 tog. Fasten off.
Rejoin yarn at centre edge of rem 45/48/51 sts.

### RIGHT HALF FRONT

*Row 1*: K.
*Row 2*: Cast off 4 sts, p to end of row.
*Row 3*: K to last 4 sts, k2 tog, k2.
*Row 4*: P.
Dec 1 st at armhole edge on next row and every foll alt row, at the same time dec 1 st at neck edge on next row and every foll 4th row until 4 sts rem.
*Next row*: P.
*Next row*: K2 tog, k2.
*Next row*: P.
*Next row*: K2 tog, k1.
*Next row*: P2 tog. Fasten off.

### SLEEVES (both alike)

With 4½ mm ndls cast on 40/44/44 sts. Work in k2, p2 rib for 6.5 cm (2½ in).
Change to 5½ mm ndls.
Cont in st st and work 4 rows, then inc 1 st at each end of next row and every foll 6th row until there are 60/64/66 sts.
Cont straight in st st until sleeve measures 46 cm (16½ in) from cast-on edge, ending with a p row.

### Shape raglan top

Cast off 4 sts at beg of next 2 rows.
St st 4 rows.
*Next row*: K2, skpo, k to last 4 sts, k2 tog, k2.
St st 3 rows straight.
Cont decreasing in this way on next row and every foll 4th row until 42/46/48 sts rem.
P one row.
Dec as before at each end of next row and every foll alt row until 8/10/10 sts rem.
Leave sts on a spare ndl.

## NECK INSET

With 5 mm ndls cast on 2 sts.
*Row 1* (right side): K1, KFB.
*Row 2*: K1, p1, PFB.
*Row 3*: P1, k2, p1.
*Row 4*: K1, p2, KFB.
*Row 5*: P2, k2, PFB.
*Row 6*: K2, p2, k2.
*Row 7*: P2, k2, p1, PFB.
*Row 8*: P1, k2, p2, k1, KFB.
*Row 9*: K1, p2, k2, p2, k1.
Cont in this way increasing 1 st at end only on 2 rows out of 3 rows, working extra sts in k2, p2 rib until there are 28/32/36 sts.

**Shape neck**
*Row 1* (right side): Rib 7 sts, turn; leaving rem sts on spare ndl. ****
*Row 2*: Sl.1, rib to end.
*Row 3*: Rib 5 sts, turn.
*Row 4*: Sl.1, rib to last st, inc into last st.
*Row 5*: Rib 4 sts, turn.
*Row 6*: Sl.1, rib to last st, inc into last st.
*Row 7*: Rib 3 sts, turn.
*Row 8*: Sl.1, rib 2 sts.
*Row 9*: Small and large size only: K1 turn. Medium size only: P1, turn.
*Row 10*: Small and large size only: PFB. Medium size only: KFB.
Cut yarn and leave these 10/10/10 shaping sts on a spare ndl.
Return to sts left on spare ndl at **** and sl next (centre) 10/14/18 sts on to a st-holder.
Rejoin yarn at centre edge to rem 11 sts and work as follows:
*Row 1*: Rib 11 sts.
*Row 2*: Rib 9 sts, turn.
*Row 3*: Sl.1, rib to last st, inc into last st.
*Row 4*: Rib 8 sts, turn.
*Row 5*: Sl.1, rib to last st, inc into last st.
*Row 6*: Rib 7 sts, turn.
*Row 7*: Sl.1, rib to end.
*Row 8*: Rib 5 sts, turn.
*Row 9*: Sl.1, rib to last st, inc into last st.
*Row 10*: Rib 4 sts, turn.
*Row 11*: Sl.1, rib to last st, inc into last st.

*Row 12*: Rib 3 sts, turn.
*Row 13*: Sl.1, rib 2 sts.
*Row 14*: Small and large sizes only: K1, turn. Medium size only: P1, turn.
*Row 15*: Small and large sizes only: PFB. Medium size only: KFB.
*Row 16* (all sizes): Rib 16.
Leave these 16/16/16 shaping sts on a spare ndl.

## BUTTONHOLE BAND

With 4½ mm ndls cast on 2 sts.
*Row 1*: K1, KFB.
*Row 2*: KFB, p2.
*Row 3*: K2, p1, PFB.
*Row 4*: PFB, k2, p2.
*Row 5*: K2, p2, k2.
*Row 6*: P2, k2, p2.
Rep rows 5 and 6 one/three/one times more.
*1st buttonhole row*: K2, cast off 2, (1 st on ndl), k1.
*2nd buttonhole row*: P2, cast on 2 sts over those cast off to complete buttonhole, p2.
** Rib 10/10/12 rows, then rep the 2 buttonhole rows again. **
Rep from ** to ** 3 times more (5 buttonholes made).
Rib 4/4/6 rows. Leave these sts on spare ndl.

## BUTTON BAND

Work same length as buttonhole band, omitting buttonholes.

*To Make Up*

Do not press. Sew row ends of buttonhole band to row ends of neck inset, placing shortest side of buttonhole band to shortest side of inset (the band will be about 4 cm (1½ in) above inset at top). Fit inset with buttonhole band into V neck of front of sweater, placing point of band into base of V and inset on right side of neck up to about 1 cm (½ in) from top of sweater; stitch neatly in place leaving buttonhole band side open. Sew button band to other side of front of sweater, longest side of band to left side of neck. Join side seams from top of ribbing 15 cm (6 in) from cast-on edge to underarms, using a fine backstitch. Set in sleeves and join sleeve seams.

## NECKBAND

With 4½ mm ndls and right side of work facing, k2, p2, k2 across buttonhole band sts left on spare ndl, pick up and k6/8/6 sts from left side of neck along row ends of buttonhole band, rib across the 10/10/10 shaping sts from spare ndl, then rib across centre front 10/14/18 sts from st-holder, rib across the 16/16/16 shaping sts from spare ndl at other side of neck, pick up and k3/3/3 sts from right side of neck on sweater.
*Small size only*: work across top of sleeve thus: p1, k2, p2, k2, p1; then across back neck sts thus: p1, * k1, KFB, p1, k2, p2; rep from * ending k1, KFB, p1; after which work across sleeve top sts and button band sts thus: ** k2, p2; rep from ** ending k2.
*Medium size only*: work across top of sleeve sts thus: k1, (p2, k2) twice, p1; then across back neck sts thus: p1, * k1, KFB, p1, k2, p2; rep from * ending k1, KFB, p1, k2; after which work across sleeve top sts and button band sts thus: ** p2, k2; rep from ** to end.
*Large size only*: work across top of sleeve sts thus: p1, (k2, p2) twice, k1, then across back neck sts thus: k1, * p2, k1, KFB, p1, k2; rep from * to end, after which work across sleeve top sts and button band sts thus: ** p2, k2; rep from ** to end.
Now work in rib for ALL sizes as follows:
*Row 1*: * P2, k2; rep from * to last 2 sts, p2.

*Row 2*: * K2, p2; rep from * to last 2 sts, k2.
Rep rows 1 and 2 once more.
Change to 5 mm ndls. Rep row 1 once more.
*1st buttonhole row*: K2, cast off 2, rib to end.
*2nd buttonhole row*: Rib, casting on 2 sts over those cast off to complete buttonhole.
Change to 5½ mm ndls. Rib 2 rows. Cast off in rib.
Sew on 6 buttons to correspond with buttonholes.

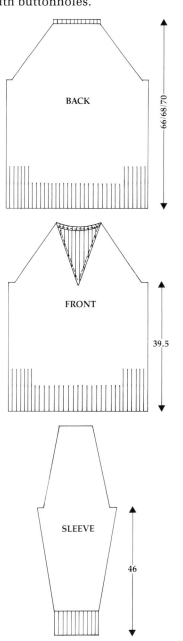

BACK

66/68/70

FRONT

39.5

SLEEVE

46

# Skipper

## Stitches used

Mainly in toggle knot cable pattern on a background of reversed stocking stitch. Two-and-two rib for welts, cuffs and collar.

## Sizes

Medium/large – to suit bust size 91–97/102–107 cm (36–38/40–42 in); length from shoulder 68/69 cm (26¾/27 in); sleeve seam 46/46 cm (18/18 in).

## Materials

Twenty-one/twenty-two 50g balls of Yarnworks Merino Sport. The quantities of yarn specified are based on average requirements and are therefore approximate.

## Needles

4½ mm (no. 7); 5½ mm (no. 5); cable needle; stitch-holders.

## Tension

22 sts and 23 rows to 10 cm (4 in) square measured over pattern on 5½ mm ndls.

## Note

It is very important that you check your tension carefully before you begin this design. The tension of the knitting controls the size of the finished garment. If your sample has less sts than our tension, try again with smaller ndls and vice versa, then work the garment with the ndls which produce our tension.
Instructions given for two sizes. The number of stitches in this pattern does not remain constant.

## Special abbreviations

DI – double increase thus: (k1 tbl and k1) into next st, then insert point of left-hand ndl behind vertical strand that runs downwards from between the 2 sts just made, then k1 tbl into this st (3 sts); C4F – cable 4 front (sl next 3 sts on to cable ndl and leave at front of work, p1, then k3 from cable ndl);
C6F – cable 6 front (sl next 3 sts on to a cable ndl and leave at front of work, k3, then k3 from cable ndl); C6B – cable 6 back (sl next 3 sts on to a cable ndl and leave at back of work, k3, then k3 from cable ndl); C5B – cable 5 back (sl next 2 sts on to cable ndl and leave at back of work, k3, then p2 from cable ndl); C7Dec – cable 7 decrease (sl next 3 sts on to a cable ndl and leave at front of work, k2 tog, k1, p1, then k3 sts from cable ndl); M1L – make 1 lifted – lift the side loop of the next st one row below on to left-hand ndl and k into front of it).

# Instructions

## BACK

With 4½ mm ndls cast on 114/118 sts. Work in rib as follows:
*Row 1:* (right side) K2, * p2, k2; rep from * to end.
*Row 2:* P2, * k2, p2; rep from * to end.
Rep last 2 rows for 10 cm (4 in), ending with a right side row.
*Inc row:* Rib 9/3, inc into next st, (rib 4/4, inc into next st) 19/21 times, rib to end. 134/140 sts.
Change to 5½ mm ndls and work as follows:
*Foundation row 1:* (right side) P6/9, * k2, p8; rep from * ending last rep with p6/9.
*Foundation row 2:* K6/9, * p2, k8; rep from * ending last rep with k6/9.
Rep last 2 rows once more.
Now work in main patt as follows:
*Row 1:* (right side) P3/6, * DI – see special abbreviations – p2, k2, p8, k2, p5; rep from * to last 11/14 sts, DI, p2, k2, p6/9.
*Row 2:* K6/9, * p2, k2, p3, k5, p2, k8; rep from * to last 10/13 sts, p2, k2, p3, k3/6.
*Row 3:* P3/6, * C4F – see special abbreviations – p1, k2, p2, DI, p5, k2, p5; rep from * to last 13/16 sts, C4F, p1, k2, p2, DI, p3/6.
*Row 4:* K3/6, * p3, k2, p2, k1, p3, k6, p2, k5; rep from * to last 15/18 sts, p3, k2, p2, k1, p3, k4/7.
*Row 5:* P4/7, * C4F, M1L – see special abbreviations – k2, C5B – see special abbreviations – p5, k2, p6; rep from * to last 14/17 sts, C4F, M1L, k2, C5B, p3/6.
*Row 6:* K5/8, * p9, k7, p2, k7; rep from * to last 14/17 sts, p9, k5/8.
*Row 7:* P5/8, * C6B – see special abbreviations – k3, p7, k2, p7; rep from * to last 14/17 sts, C6B, k3, p5/8.
*Row 8:* As row 6.
*Row 9:* P5/8, * k3, C6F, p7, k2, p7; rep from * to last 14/17 sts, k3, C6F, p5/8.
*Row 10:* As row 6.
*Row 11:* As row 7.
*Row 12:* As row 6.
*Row 13:* P3/6, * C5B, C7Dec – see special abbreviations – p6, k2, p5; rep from * to last 16/19 sts, C5B, C7Dec, p4/7.
*Row 14:* K4/7, * p3, k1, p2, k2, yfwd, sl 1, p2 tog, psso, k5, p2, k6; rep from * to last 14/17 sts, p3, k1, p2, k2, yfwd, sl 1, p2 tog, psso, k3/6.
*Row 15:* P6/9, * k2, p1, k3, p6, k2, p8; rep from * to last 10/13 sts, k2, p1, k3, p4/7.
*Row 16:* K4/7, * yfwd, sl 1, p2 tog, psso, k1, p2, k8, p2, k6; rep from * to last 12/15 sts, yfwd, sl 1, p2 tog, psso, k1, p2, k6/9.
*Row 17:* P6/9, * k2, p8; rep from * ending last rep with p6/9 instead of p8.
*Row 18:* K6/9, * p2, k8; rep from * ending last rep with k6/9, instead of k8.
*Row 19:* P6/9, * k2, p5, DI, p2, k2, p8; rep from * to last 8/11 sts, k2, p6/9.
*Row 20:* K6/9, * p2, k8, p2, k2, p3, k5; rep from * to last 8/11 sts, p2, k6/9.

*Row 21*: P6/9, * k2, p5, C4F, p1, k2, p2, DI, p5; rep from * to last 8/11 sts, k2, p6/9.
*Row 22*: K6/9, * p2, k5, p3, k2, p2, k1, p3, k6; rep from * to last 8/11 sts, p2, k6/9.
*Row 23*: P6/9, * k2, p6, C4F, M1L, k2, C5B, p5; rep from * to last 8/11 sts, k2, p6/9.
*Row 24*: K6/9, * p2, k7, p9, k7; rep from * to last 8/11 sts, p2, k6/9.
*Row 25*: P6/9, * k2, p7, C6B, k3, p7; rep from * to last 8/11 sts, k2, p6/9.
*Row 26*: As row 24.
*Row 27*: P6/9, * k2, p7, k3, C6F, p7; rep from * to last 8/11 sts, k2, p6/9.
*Row 28*: As row 24.
*Row 29*: As row 25.
*Row 30*: As row 24.
*Row 31*: P6/9, * k2, p5, C5B, C7Dec, p6; rep from * to last 8/11 sts, k2, p6/9.
*Row 32*: K6/9, * p2, k6, p3, k1, p2, k2, yfwd, sl 1, p2 tog, psso, k5; rep from * to last 8/11 sts, p2, k6/9.
*Row 33*: P6/9, * k2, p8, k2, p1, k3, p6; rep from * to last 8/11 sts, k2, p6/9.
*Row 34*: K6/9, * p2, k6, yfwd, sl 1, p2 tog, psso, k1, p2, k8; rep from * to last 8/11 sts, p2, k6/9.
*Row 35*: As row 17.
*Row 36*: As row 18.
These 36 rows form main patt. Cont in patt until 68/69 cm (26¾/27¼ in) from cast-on edge, ending with a wrong-side row.

**Shape shoulders**
Cast off 40/43 sts at beg of next 2 rows. Leave rem 54/54 sts on a st-holder.

## FRONT

Work as given for back until work measures 61 cm (24 in) from cast-on edge, ending with a wrong-side row.

### Shape neck
*Next row:* (right side) Patt 53/56, turn; leaving the rem 81/84 sts on a spare ndl.
Cont on first set of 53/56 sts thus:

## LEFT HALF FRONT

** Cast off 3 sts at beg (neck edge) of next row, after which cast off 2 sts at beg (neck edge) on foll 5 alt rows. 40/43 sts.
Work straight until front measures same as back to shoulder, ending at side edge.

### Shape shoulder
Cast off 40/43 sts. Fasten off.
Return to the rem 81/84 sts and with right side of work facing sl next 28/28 sts on to a st-holder for centre front neck, then rejoin yarn to neck edge of rem 53/56 sts and work right half front from ** on left half front to end.

## SLEEVES (both alike)

With 4½ mm ndls cast on 38/42 sts.
Work 5 cm (2 in) in rib as given for back, ending with a right-side row.
*Inc row:* (wrong side) Rib 5/5, inc into next st, (rib 1, inc into next st) 13/15 times, rib to end of row. 52/58 sts.
Change to 5½ mm ndls and work as follows:
*Foundation row 1:* (right side) P5/8, * k2, p8; rep from * ending last rep with p5/8.
*Foundation row 2:* K5/8, * p2, k8; rep from * ending last rep with k5/8.
*Foundation row 3:* Inc into first st, p4/7, * k2, p8; rep from * ending last rep with p4/7, inc into last st. 54/60 sts.

*Foundation row 4:* K6/9, * p2, k8; rep from * ending last rep with k6/9.
*Foundation row 5:* P6/9, * k2, p8; rep from * ending last rep with p6/9.
Rep foundation row 4, then work as follows:
Now work 2 rows in main patt as given for back, then cont in patt and inc 1 st at each end of next row and every foll 4th row until there are 84/90 sts, working the extra sts into patt as they are made, after which inc 1 st at each end of every foll alt row until there are 108/114 sts, still working the extra sts into patt as they are made. Cont straight until sleeve measures 46/46 cm (18/18 in) from cast-on edge, ending with a wrong-side row. Cast off loosely.

## COLLAR

Join right shoulder seam, using a fine backstitch.
With 4½ mm ndls and right side of work facing pick up and k20 sts evenly down left front neck, k the 28/28 centre front sts from st-holder, pick up and k20 sts evenly up right front neck, then k the 54/54 back neck sts from st-holder. 122 sts.
Work 15 cm (6 in) in k2, p2, rib.
Cast off loosely in rib.

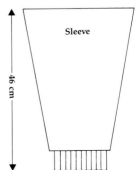

## To Make Up

Do not press. Join left shoulder seam and cont along row ends of collar, reversing seam on collar to allow for turning. Set in sleeves, placing the centre of cast-off edge of sleeve to shoulder seam. Join sleeve and side seams, using a fine backstitch.

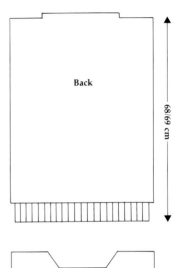

Back

68/69 cm

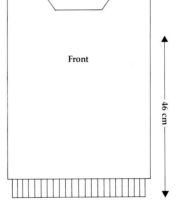

Front

46 cm

Sleeve

46 cm

## Stitches used
Mainly in stocking stitch. Welts, cuffs, neckband and collar in one-and-one rib.

## Sizes
Small/medium/large – to suit bust 86/91/97 cm (34/36/38 in); length 61 cm (24 in); sleeve seam 49 cm (19¼ in).

## Materials
Seven/seven/eight 50g balls of Yarnworks Merino Luxury Wool in main colour (dark) and six/seven/seven 50g balls in contrast colour (light).
The quantities of yarn specified are based on average requirements and are therefore approximate.

## Needles
3¼ mm (no. 10); 4½ mm (no. 7); 3¼ mm (no. 10) circular ndl 60 cm (23½ in) long; 2 st-holders.

## Tension
22 sts and 28 rows to 10 cm (4 in) square measured over stocking stitch on 4½ mm ndls.

## Note
Instructions given for three sizes.

## Special abbreviations
M – main (dark). A – contrast (light).

# Instructions

## BACK

With 3¼ mm ndls and M cast on 95/101/107 sts using thumb method.
*Row 1* (right side): K1, * p1, k1; rep from * to end.
*Row 2*: P1, * k1, p1, rep from * to end.
Rep these 2 rows until rib measures 7.5 cm (3 in) from cast-on edge, ending with row 1.
*Inc row*: Rib 9/6/9, * inc 1, rib 6/7/7, rep from * to last 9/7/10 sts, inc 1, rib to end. 107/113/119 sts.
Change to 4½ mm ndls.
Cont in st st, beg with a k row and stripe sequence of 15 rows in A yarn and 15 rows in M yarn until 150 rows in all have been worked. Back should measure 61 cm (24 in) from cast-on edge.

### Shape shoulders
With M yarn, cast off 34/36/38 sts at beg of next 2 rows. Sl rem 39/41/43 sts on to a st-holder.

## FRONT

Work as back until 135 rows in all have been worked.
Cont in M yarn only. Shape neck.
*Next row*: P42/44/46 sts, turn; leave rem sts on a spare ndl.
Cont on first set of sts for right half front. Dec 1 st at neck edge on next 4 rows then on foll 4 alt rows. Work 3 rows. Cast off rem 34/36/38 sts.
With wrong side of work facing, sl first 23/25/27 sts from spare ndl on to a st-holder and leave for centre front neck, rejoin M yarn to rem sts and p to end.
Dec 1 st at neck edge on next 4 rows then on 4 foll alt rows. Work 2 rows.
Cast off rem 34/36/38 sts.

## SLEEVES (both alike)

With 3¼ mm ndls and M yarn cast on 45/47/47 sts.
Work in rib as given for back welt for 8 cm (3 in), ending with row 1.
*Inc row*: Rib 4/5/5, * inc 1, rib 3; rep from * to last 1/2/2 sts, rib to end. 55/57/57 sts.
Change to 4½ mm ndls.
Cont in st st and stripe sequence as given for back, inc 1 st inside the first and last st on 3rd row and every foll 5th row until there are 85/87/87 sts then on every foll 4th row until there are 105/107/107 sts. Work 7 rows straight.

Work should measure 49 cm (19¼ in) from cast-on edge. With M yarn, cast off loosely.

## NECKBAND

Join right shoulder seam.
With A yarn, 3¼ mm ndls and right side of work facing, pick up and k 15 sts down shaped edge of left front neck, k the 23/25/27 sts from st-holder at centre front neck, pick up and k 16 sts up shaped edge of right front neck to shoulder, k the 39/41/43 sts from st-holder at centre back neck. 93/97/101 sts.
Work 7 rows in rib as given for back welt, beg with row 2. Cast off in rib. Join left shoulder and neckband seam.

## COLLAR

With A yarn, circular ndl 3¼ mm, right side facing and beg at centre front inside the neckband, pick up (from base of neckband) and k 30/31/32 sts from right front neck to shoulder, 43/45/47 sts from back neck and 30/31/32 sts from left front neck to centre. 103/107/111 sts.
Working backwards and forwards, work 7 rows in rib as given for back welt, beg with row 1.
Change to 4½ mm ndls and cont in rib until collar measures 8 cm (3¼ in) from pick up edge, ending with row 2.
Cast off in rib.

# To Make Up

Join side and sleeve seams using a fine back stitch. Set in sleeves. Join first 5 rows of collar at centre front. Turn collar to right side.

## Stitches used

One-and-one rib for welts, cuffs and collar. Mainly in a simple mock rib pattern. Front yoke worked in Fair Isle in stocking stitch.

## Size

Medium – to suit chest 107 to 112 cm (42 to 44 in); length from shoulder 64 cm (25 in); sleeve seam 47 cm (18½ in).

## Materials

Twelve 50g balls of Yarnworks Merino Luxury Wool in main colour, two 50g balls of the same yarn in 1st contrast A, and 1 ball each of 2nd and 3rd contrasts.
The quantities of yarn specified are based on average requirements and are therefore approximate.

## Needles

3¼ mm (no. 10); 4½ mm (no. 7); 5 mm (no. 6).

## Tension

24 sts and 32 rows to 10 cm (4 in) square measured over mock rib pattern on 5 mm ndls.

## Note

Instructions given for one size.

## Special abbreviations

MC – main colour; A – 1st contrast; B – 2nd contrast; C – 3rd contrast.

# Instructions

## BACK

With 3¼ mm ndls and MC cast on 131 sts.
*Row 1* (right side): K1, * p1, k1; rep from * to end.
*Row 2*: P1, * k1, p1; rep from * to end.
Rep last 2 rows for 6.5 cm (2½ in).
*Inc row*: P and inc 10 sts evenly across row. 141 sts.
Change to 5 mm ndls and work in mock rib patt as follows:
*Row 1* (right side): K.
*Row 2*: K1, * yf, sl.1, yb, k1; rep from * to end.
These 2 rows form rib patt. Rep them until back measures 63.5 cm (25 in) from cast-on edge.
Cast off right across, taking tog every 13th and 14th st.

## FRONT

Work as given for back until front measures 27 cm (10½ in) from cast-on edge, ending with a wrong-side row.
Divide for neck thus:
*Next row* (right side): K70, turn leaving the rem 71 sts on a spare ndl.

## LEFT HALF FRONT

** *Row 1*: K2 tog (neck edge), work to end.
*Row 2*: Work without dec.
*Row 3*: K2 tog, work to end.
*Row 4*: Work to last 2 sts k2 tog (neck edge).
*Row 5*: Work without dec.
*Row 6*: Work to last 2 sts, k2 tog.
Rep last 6 rows twice more and the first 3 rows again.
Cont decreasing at neck edge and beg raglan armhole shaping as follows:
*Row 1*: Cast off 2 sts (armhole edge), work to last 2 sts, k2 tog (neck edge).
*Row 2*: Work to last 2 sts, k2 tog.

*Row 3*: K2 tog, work to last 2 sts, k2 tog.
*Row 4*: K2 tog, work to last 2 sts, k2 tog.
*Row 5*: K2 tog, work to end.
*Row 6*: K2 tog, work to last 2 sts, k2 tog.
*Row 7*: K2 tog, work to last 2 sts, k2 tog.
Rep from row 2 to row 7 until 3 sts rem. K3 tog and fasten off.
Return to rem 71 sts and with right side of work facing rejoin yarn at neck edge, k2 tog, then k to end. 70 sts.

## RIGHT HALF FRONT

Work one row back to neck edge, then rep from ** on left half front to end.

## LEFT SLEEVE

With 3¼ mm ndls and MC cast on 57 sts.
Work 6.5 cm (2½ in) in k1, p1 rib as given for back.
Change to 5 mm ndls and work 6 rows in mock rib patt as for back, then inc 1 st at each end of next row and every foll 3rd row until there are 131 sts, working extra sts in patt as they are made.
Work straight until sleeve measures 47 cm (18½ in) from cast-on edge, ending with a wrong-side row. (End with a right-side row here on right sleeve.)

### Shape top

*Row 1*: Cast off 65 sts (this forms depths of armhole on back), work to end of row.
*Row 2*: K2 tog, work to end.
*Row 3*: K2 tog, work to end.
*Row 4*: K2 tog, work to end.
*Row 5*: K2 tog, work to last 2 sts, k2 tog.
*Row 6*: Work without dec.
*Row 7*: K2 tog, work to last 2 sts, k2 tog.
*Row 8*: K2 tog, work to end.
*Row 9*: K2 tog, work to end.

*Row 10*: K2 tog, work to end.
*Row 11*: K2 tog, work to last 2 sts, k2 tog.
*Row 12*: Work without dec.
Now cont in mock rib patt and dec 1 st at beg (inside edge) of next row and this edge on foll 32 rows, at the same time dec 1 st at outside edge (raglan edge) as follows: (dec 1 st on next 2 rows, work one row straight) 3 times, after which dec 1 st at raglan edge on every foll alt row 13 times. Fasten off.

## RIGHT SLEEVE

Work as left sleeve, reversing all shapings and noting item in brackets so that row 1 of raglan shaping is a wrong side row when casting off 65 sts.

## FAIR ISLE YOKE

Begin by joining the front raglan sides of sleeves to the raglan shaping of main part of front. With right side of work facing and using a 4½ mm ndl pick up 109 sts from shaped edge of left sleeve top and down shaped edge of main part of front to centre point of V, pick up 1 st at centre point of V and mark this st, then pick up 109 sts up shaped edge of right front edge and right sleeve edge. 219 sts.
*Next row* (wrong side): With MC p.
Now begin the Fair Isle patt, joining in and breaking off the colours as required.
*Row 1* (right side): With B, k.
*Row 2*: P1 A, * p1 B, p1 A; rep from * to end.
*Row 3*: With A, k2 tog, k104, k3 tog, k1 (marked st), k3 tog tbl, k to last 2 sts, k2 tog.
*Row 4*: P1 A, p3 MC, * p3 A, p1 C, p3 A, p5 MC; ** rep from * to ** 7 times more, p13 A, p5 MC, now rep from * to ** 7 times, then p3 A, p1 C, p3 A, p3 MC, p1 A.
*Row 5*: K2 tog MC, k1 MC, * k3 A, k3 C, k3 A, k3 MC, ** rep from * to ** 7 times more, k4 A, k3 tog A, k1

A (marked st), k3 tog tb1 A, k4 A, k3 MC, now rep from * to ** 7 times, k3 A, k3 C, k3 A, k1 MC, k2 tog MC.
*Row 6*: P1 MC, * p3 A, p5 C, p3 A, p1 MC, ** rep from * to ** 7 times more, p13 A, p1 MC, now rep from * to ** 7 times, p3 A, p5 C, p3 A, p1 MC.
*Row 7*: With A, k2 tog, k98, k3 tog, k1 (marked st), k3 tog tbl, k98, k2 tog.
*Row 8*: P1 A, * p1 C, p3 A, p1 B, p3 A, p1 C, p3 A; ** rep from * to ** 6 times more, p1 C, p3 A, p1 B, p3 A, p1 C, p13 A, now rep from * to ** 7 times, then p1 C, p3 A, p1 B, p3 A, p1 C, p1 A.
*Row 9*: K2 tog C, * k2 A, k3 B, k2 A, k1 C, k3 A, k1 C, ** rep from * to ** 6 times more, k2 A, k3 B, k2 A, k1 C, k3 A, k3 tog A, k1 A (marked st), k3 tog tbl A, k3 A, k1 C, then rep from * to ** 7 times, k2 A, k3 B, k2 A, k2 tog C.
*Row 10*: P2 A, * p2 B, p1 A, p2 B, p2 A, p1 C, p1 A, p1 C, p2 A, ** rep from * to ** 6 times more, p2 B, p1 A, p2 B, p13 A, then rep from * to ** 7 times, p2 B, p1 A, p2 B, p2 A.
*Row 11*: K2 tog B, k1 B, * k3 A, k2 B, k2 A, k1 C, k2 A, k2 B, ** rep from * to ** 6 times more, k3 A, k2 B, k2 A, k3 tog A, k1 A (marked st), k3 tog tbl A, k2 A, k2 B, then rep from * to ** 7 times, k3 A, k1 B, k2 tog B.
*Row 12*: P2 B, * p3 A, p3 B, p1 A, p1 C, p1 A, p3 B, ** rep from * to ** 6 times more, p17 A, p3 B, p1 A, p1 C, p1 A, p3 B, rep from * to ** 6 times, p3 A, p2 B.
*Row 13*: K2 tog A, * k3 C, k4 A, k1 C, k4 A, ** rep from * to ** 6 times more, k3 C, k2 A, k3 tog A, k1 A (marked st), k3 tog tbl A, k2 A, then rep from * to ** 7 times, k3 C, k2 tog A.
*Row 14*: With MC p88, p7 A, then with MC p to end of row.
*Row 15*: K2 tog C, k2 C, * k4 A, k1 C, k4 A, k3 C, ** rep from * to ** 5 times more, k4 A, k1 C, k7 A, k3 tog A, k1 A (marked st), k3 tog A, k7 A, k1 C, k4 A, k3 C then rep from * to ** 5 times, k4 A, k1 C, k4 A, k2 C, k2 tog C.

*Row 16*: P3 A, * p3 B, p1 A, p1 C, p1 A, p3 B, p3 A, ** rep from * to ** 5 times more, p3 B, p1 A, p1 C, p17 A, p1 C, p1 A, p3 B, p3 A, now rep from * to ** 6 times.
*Row 17*: K2 tog A, k1 A, * k2 B, k2 A, k1 C, k2 A, k2 B, k3 A, ** rep from * to ** 5 times more, k2 B, k2 A, k1 C, k5 A, k3 tog A, k1 A (marked st), k3 tog tbl A, k5 A, k1 C, k2 A, k2 B, k3 A, then rep from * to ** 5 times, k2 B, k2 A, k1 C, k2 A, k2 B, k1 A, k2 tog A.
*Row 18*: P1 A, * p2 B, p2 A, p1 C, p1 A, p1 C, p2 A, p2 B, p1 A, ** rep from * to ** 5 times more, p2 B, p2 A, p1 C, p1 A, p1 C, p11 A, p1 C, p1 A, p1 C, p2 A, p2 B, p1 A, then rep from * to ** 6 times.
*Row 19*: K2 tog B, * k2 A, k1 C, k3 A, k1 C, k2 A, k3 B, ** rep from * to ** 5 times more, k2 A, k1 C, k5 A, k3 tog A, k1 A (marked st), k3 tog tbl A, k5 A, k1 C, k2 A, k3 B, then rep from * to ** 5 times, k2 A, k1 C, k3 A, k1 C, k2 A, k2 tog B.
*Row 20*: P3 A, * p1 C, p3 A, p1 C, p3 A, p1 B, p3 A, ** rep from * to ** 5 times more, p1 C, p13 A, p1 C, p3 A, p1 B, p3 A, then rep from * to ** 5 times, (p1 C, p3 A) twice.
*Row 21*: With A k2 tog, k77, k3 tog, k1 (marked st), k3 tog tbl, k to last 2 sts, k2 tog.
*Row 22*: P1 C, * p3 A, p1 MC, p3 A, p5 C, ** rep from * to ** 5 times more, p13 A, p5 C, then rep from * to ** 5 times, p3 A, p1 MC, p3 A, p1 C.
*Row 23*: K2 tog A, k1 A, * k3 MC, k3 A, k3 C, k3 A, ** rep from * to ** 4 times more, k3 MC, k3 A, k3 C, k4 A, then k3 tog A, k1 A (marked st), k3 tog tbl A, k4 A, k3 C, k3 A, then rep from * to ** 5 times, k3 MC, k1 A, k2 tog A.
*Row 24*: P1 A, * p5 MC, p3 A, p1 C, p3 A, ** rep from * to ** 4 times more, p5 MC, p3 A, p1 C, p13 A, p1 C, p3 A, then rep from * to ** 5 times, p5 MC, p1 A.
*Row 25*: With A k2 tog, k71, k3 tog, k1 (marked st), k3 tog tbl, k to last 2 sts, k2 tog.
*Row 26*: (P1 A, p1 B) 35 times, p7 A, (p1 B, p1 A) 35 times.
*Row 27*: With B k2 tog, k68, k3 tog

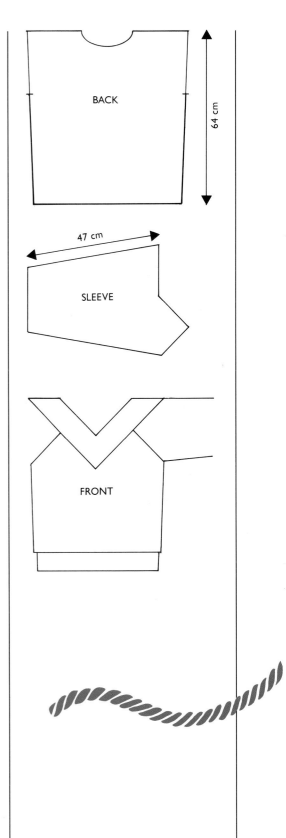

BACK

64 cm

47 cm

SLEEVE

FRONT

A, k1 A (marked st), k3 tog tbl A, with B k to last 2 sts, k2 tog B. 141 sts.
Cast off with a size finer ndl.
Press Fair Isle yoke carefully as instructed on ball band, avoiding the mock rib patt of main part of sweater.

## COLLAR

With 3¼ mm ndls and MC cast on 90 sts.
Work in k1, p1 rib and shape sides by casting on 4 sts at beg of next 36 rows. 234 sts.
Work 4 cm (1¾ in) straight, then cast off in rib.

## To Make Up

Do not press. Join sleeve and side seams, using a fine backstitch. Sew cast-off edge of back sleeve top from shoulder of back to beg of raglan shaping on front. Pin cast-on edge of collar to neck edge of sweater, placing centre of collar to centre back neck edge, and cont down to point of V, lapping left front over right and join the 4 cm (1¾ in) straight edge of left side to slope of right front of sweater and the right straight edge of collar to go underneath the left front slope of sweater. Sew neatly in place. Turn back shawl collar.

# James

## Stitches used

Mainly in fisherman rib. Welt and cuffs in one-and-one rib.

## Sizes

Small to extra large to suit chest sizes 91/97/102/107/112/117 cm (36/38/40/42/44/46 in). Length from shoulder 62/64/64/65/65/66 cm (24½/25/25/25½/25½/26 in). Sleeve seam 48 cm (19 in).

## Materials

Fourteen / fifteen / fifteen / sixteen / sixteen / sixteen 50g balls Yarnworks Merino Luxury Wool. The quantities of yarn specified are based on average requirements and are therefore approximate.

## Needles

1 pair size 3¼ mm (no. 10), 3¾ mm (no. 9) and 5½ mm (no. 8).

## Tension

17 sts and 38 rows to 10 cm (4 in) square measured over fisherman rib on 5½ mm ndls.

## Instructions

### BACK

With 3¼ mm ndls cast on 87 (91/95/99/103/107) sts.
*Row 1* (right side): Sl 1, k1, * p1, k1, rep from * to last st, k1.
*Row 2*: Sl 1, * p1, k1, rep from * to end.
These 2 rows form rib.
Cont until work measures 7.5 cm (3 in) from beg, ending with a wrong side row.
Change to 5½ mm ndls.

*Row 1* (right side): Sl 1, k1 below, * p1, k1 below, rep from * to last st, k1.
*Row 2*: Sl 1, * p1, k1 below; rep from * to last 2 sts, p1, k1.
These 2 rows form fisherman rib.
Cont in fisherman rib until work measures 38 cm (15 in) from beg, ending with a wrong side row.

### Shape armholes

Keeping fisherman rib correct work 20 rows, dec 1 st at each end of next row and every foll alt row. 67 (71/75/79/83/87) sts.
Cast off in rib.

### FRONT

Work as back.

### SLEEVES AND YOKE

(Worked in one piece.)
With 3¼ mm ndls cast on 47 (51/51/55/55/59) sts and work 7.5 cm (3 in) in rib as given for back, ending with a wrong side row.
Change to 5½ mm ndls and work in fisherman rib as given for back, inc 1 st at each end of 7th row and every foll 6th row until 87 (91/91/95/95/99) sts are on needle.
Work 21 rows straight.

### Shape yoke

Keeping fisherman rib correct work 20 rows dec 1 st at each end of next row and every foll alt row until 67 (71/71/75/75/79) sts rem.
Place a marker at each end of last row.
Work 50 (54/60/60/66/70) rows straight.

### Shape neck

*Next row*: Patt 33 (35/35/37/37/39) sts, cast off next 3(5/5/5/5/7) sts, patt to end.
*Next row*: Patt 31 (31/31/33/33/33) sts, turn and leave rem sts on a spare needle.
Cont on these 31 (31/31/33/33/33)

sts only for front neck.
Keeping fisherman rib correct dec 1 st at beg of next row and every alt row until 11 sts rem.
Cast off loosely in rib. This edge to measure 7.5 cm (3 in).
With 4½ mm ndls cast on 11 sts loosely to measure 7.5 cm (3 in) to match cast-off edge and work 1 row in rib as given for back.
Beg with row 2 work in fisherman rib inc 1 st at end of next row and every foll alt row until 31 (31/31/33/33/33) sts are on needle, ending with a wrong side row.
Break off yarn, leave these sts on a spare needle for right side of front neck.
With wrong side facing, rejoin yarn to rem 33 (35/35/37/37/39) sts for back neck and patt to end.
Work 14 rows dec 1 st at end of next row and every foll 4th row. 29 (31/31/33/33/35) sts.
Work 26 (26/26/30/30/30) rows straight.
Work 14 rows inc 1 st at end of next row and every foll alt row. 33 (35/35/37/37/39) sts.
*Next row*: Patt to end, cast on 3 (5/5/5/5/7) sts, then patt across 31 (31/31/33/33/33) sts left on spare needle. 67 (71/71/75/75/79) sts.
Work 51 (55/61/61/67/71) rows straight.
Place a marker at each end of last row.
Keeping fisherman rib correct, work 20 rows inc 1 st at each end of next row and every foll alt row. 87 (91/91/95/95/99) sts.
Work 21 rows straight.
Dec 1 st at each end of next row and every foll 6th row until 47 (51/51/55/55/59) sts rem.
Work 7 rows straight.
Change to 3¼ mm ndls and beg with row 1 work 7.5 cm (3 in) in rib as given for back.
Cast off in rib.

## COLLAR

With right side facing and 3¾ mm ndls, pick up and k18 sts from 11 cast-on sts at right side of front neck, 48 (48/48/52/52/52) sts from shaped edge of right side of neck, 59 (59/59/63/63/63) sts from back neck, 48 (48/48/52/52/52) sts from shaped edge of left side of neck and 18 sts from 11 cast off sts. 191 (191/191/203/203/203) sts.
Beg with row 1 work 2 rows in rib as given for back.

**Shape collar**
*Rows 1 and 2*: Patt to last 6 sts, turn.
*Rows 3 and 4*: Patt to last 9 sts, turn.
*Rows 5 and 6*: Patt to last 12 sts, turn.
Work 30 rows more in rib working 3 sts less as before on every alt row. 79 sts rem.
*Next row*: Rib across all sts.
Cast off loosely in rib.

## To Make Up

Placing left side over right side for 6 cm (2½ in) sew edges together at centre front. Sew cast-off edge of back and front between markers. Sew raglan seams. Sew side and sleeve seams.

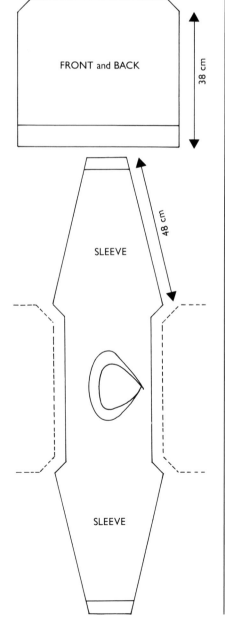

# Two Tone

SPECKLED EFFECT IS ACHIEVED BY KNITTING WITH GREEN AND BLACK WOOL TOGETHER

## Stitches used
Mainly stocking stitch. Welts, cuffs and neckband in striped rib.

## Sizes
Small/medium/large – to suit bust 86/91/97 cm (34/36/38 in); length 75 cm (29½ in); sleeve seam 46 cm (18 in).

## Materials
Nine/ten/eleven 50g balls of Yarnworks Merino Luxury Wool in main colour and nine/ten/eleven 50g balls of the same yarn in contrast colour.
The quantities of yarn specified are based on average requirements and are therefore approximate.

## Needles
6½ mm (no. 3); 8 mm (no. 0); 4½ mm (no. 7).

## Tension
13 sts and 18 rows to 10 cm (4 in) square measured over stocking stitch on 8 mm needles using 2 strands of yarn together.

## Note
Instructions given for three sizes.

## Special abbreviations
M – main colour (dark), A – contrast (light).

## Instructions

### BACK

With 6½ mm ndls and using 2 strands of M yarn cast on 71/75/79 sts using thumb method.
Using 2 strands of M yarn tog and 2 strands of A yarn tog, work as follows:
**Row 1 (right side): P1 M, M yb, * k1 A, M yf, p1 M, M yb; rep from * to end.

Row 2: K1 M, M yf, * p1 A, M yb, k1 M, M yf; rep from * to end.
Rep these 2 rows once more.
Row 5: K1 M, * 1 A, 1 M; rep from * to end.
Row 6: P1 M, * 1 A, 1 M; rep from * to end **.
Rep rows 5 and 6 until work measures 13 cm (5 in) from cast-on edge, ending with row 6. Change to 8 mm ndls and use 1 strand of M yarn and 1 strand of A yarn tog throughout.
Inc row: K5/7/6, * inc 1, k9/9/10;

rep from * to last 6/8/7 sts, inc 1, k to end. 78/82/86 sts.
Cont in st st, beg with a p row until work measures 72.5 cm (28½ in) from cast-on edge, ending with a p row.

### Shape shoulders

Cast off 12/13/14 sts at beg of next 2 rows and 12/12/13 sts at beg of foll 2 rows. Cast off rem 30/32/32 sts.

### FRONT

Work as back until front measures 6 rows less than back to shoulders, thus ending with a p row.

### Shape neck

*Next row*: K31/32/34 sts, turn; leave the rem sts on a spare ndl. Cont on first set of sts for left half front. Dec 1 st at neck edge on next 5 rows. 26/27/29 sts.

### Shape shoulder

*Next row*: Cast off 12/13/14 sts, k to last 2 sts, dec 1.
*Next row*: Dec 1, p to end.
Cast off rem 12/12/13 sts.
With right side of work facing, rejoin yarn to rem sts, cast off first 16/18/18 sts, k to end.
Dec 1 st at neck edge on next 6 rows. 25/26/28 sts.

### Shape shoulder

*Next row*: Cast off 12/13/14 sts, p to last 2 sts, dec 1.
Work 1 row. Cast off rem 12/12/13 sts.

### SLEEVES (both alike)

With 6½ mm ndls and using 2 strands of M yarn tog cast on 29 sts. Work as given for back from ** to **
Rep rows 3 and 4 until work measures 5 cm (2 in) from cast-on edge,

ending with row 4.
Change to 8 mm ndls and use 1 strand of M yarn and 1 strand of A yarn tog throughout.
*Inc row*: K5, * inc 1, k3; rep from * to end. 35 sts.
Cont in st st, beg with a p row and inc 1 st at both ends of every foll 3rd row until there are 65 sts then on every foll 4th row until there are 73 sts. Cont straight until sleeve measures 46 cm (18 in) from cast-on edge, ending with a p row. Cast off loosely.

### NECKBAND

First join right shoulder seam.
With 1 strand of M yarn, 4½ mm ndls and right side facing, pick up and k20/22/22 sts from shaped edge of left front neck, 32/36/36 sts from centre front neck, pick up and k 20/22/22 sts from shaped edge of right front neck to shoulder and 60/64/64 sts from centre back neck. 132/144/144 sts.
Use 1 strand of each yarn.
*Next row* (wrong side): * P1 M, 1 A; rep from * to end.
*Next row*: * K1 A, 1 M; rep from * to end.
Rep these 2 rows until neckband measures 6 cm (2½ in), ending with a p row. Cast off loosely.

*To Make Up*

Join left shoulder seam. Fold neckband in half to wrong side and slip cast-off edge neatly to neck on wrong side. Measure 28 cm (11 in) down from shoulders on back and front and mark with pins. Set in sleeves between pins. Join side and sleeve seams using a fine backstitch.

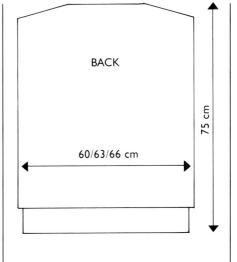

BACK

75 cm

60/63/66 cm

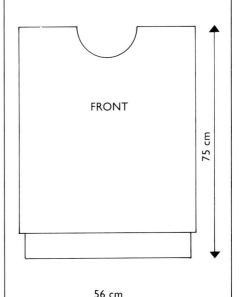

FRONT

75 cm

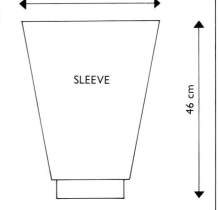

56 cm

SLEEVE

46 cm

## Stitches used

Mainly in stocking stitch and colour pattern. Welts and cuffs in one-and-one rib. Front bands, pocket tops and collar in garter stitch.

## Sizes

Small/medium/large/extra large – to suit bust or chest sizes 91/97/102/107 cm (36/38/40/42 in); length 65/66/67/68 cm (25½/26/26¼/26¾ in); sleeve seam 46/48/50/52 cm (18/19/19¾/20½ in).

## Materials

Thirteen/thirteen/fourteen/fourteen 50g balls of Yarnworks Merino Sport in main colour. Two 50g balls of same yarn in 1st contrast and 1 ball each of four other contrasts all sizes; 8 buttons. The quantities of yarn specified are based on average requirements and are therefore approximate.

## Needles

4½ mm (no. 7); 5½ mm (no. 5).

## Tension

17 sts and 21 rows to 10 cm (4 in) measured over stocking stitch on 5½ mm ndls.

## Note

Use short lengths of A yarn when working bodice pattern and a separate ball of M yarn for front bands when working yoke pattern, twist yarns together on wrong side to avoid a hole. Carry yarn not in use loosely across wrong side of work over not more than 5 sts at the time when working yoke pattern.
When working from chart, read odd-numbers (k) rows from right to left and even-numbered (p) rows from left to right.

## Special abbreviations

M – main colour; A – 1st contrast; B – 2nd contrast; C – 3rd contrast; D – 4th contrast; E – 5th contrast.

# Instructions

## BACK

With 4½ mm ndls and M yarn, cast on 96/100/104/108 sts using thumb method. Work 20 rows in k1, p1 rib.
Change to 5½ mm ndls.
Work in st st beg with a k row and patt from chart for back until row 82 of chart has been worked.

**Shape raglan armholes**
Cont in patt from chart, cast off 7 sts at beg of next 2 rows. Dec 1 st at both ends of next row and every foll alt row until 42/46/48/52 sts rem then at both ends of every row until 32/32/34/34 sts rem. Cast off.

## POCKET LININGS (make 2)

With 5½ mm ndls and M yarn, cast on 22 sts.
Work 27 rows in st st, beg with a k row.
Leave sts on spare ndl.

## RIGHT FRONT

With 4½ mm ndls and M yarn, cast on 52/54/56/58 sts using thumb method.
Row 1 (right side): K6, * k1, p1; rep from * to end.
Row 2: * K1, p1; rep from * to last 6 sts, k6.

## WOMAN'S VERSION

Rep last 2 rows once more.
1st buttonhole row: K2, cast off 2, k2 (including st used in casting off), rib to end.
2nd buttonhole row: Rib to last 4 sts, k2, cast on 2, k2.
Rep rows (1 and 2) 7 times more.

## MAN'S VERSION

Rep last 2 rows 9 times more.

## BOTH VERSIONS

Change to 5½ mm ndls.
Keeping the 6 sts at front edge in g-st and remainder in st st beg with a k row, work in patt from chart for right front making buttonholes as before on woman's version only as indicated on chart until row 22 of chart has been worked.
Place pocket as follows:
Next row: Patt 12, with M p22, patt to end.
Next row: Patt 18/20/22/24, with M p22, patt to end.
Rep last 2 rows once more.
Next row: Patt 12, with M, cast off 22 sts purlwise, patt to end.
Next row: Patt 18/20/22/24, then patt across 22 pocket lining sts, patt to end.
Keeping the 6 sts at front edge in g-st and remainder in st st and making buttonholes on woman's version only, cont in patt from chart until row 83 of chart has been worked.

**Shape raglan armhole**
Cont in patt from chart, cast off 7 sts at beg of next row. Dec 1 st at end of next row and every foll alt row until 31/33/35/37 sts rem, ending with a wrong side row.

**Shape neck**
Next row: Cast off 12 sts, patt to last 2 sts, work 2 tog.
Patt 1 row.
** Cont to dec at raglan edge on next row and every foll alt row at the same time dec 1 st at neck edge on next 3 rows then on foll 2/2/3/3 alt rows.
Keeping neck edge straight, cont to dec at raglan edge on foll alt row then on every row until 3 sts rem. Cast off. **

## LEFT FRONT

With 4½ mm ndls and M yarn, cast on 52/54/56/58 sts using thumb method.
*Row 1* (right side): * P1, k1; rep from * to last 6 sts, k6.
*Row 2*: K6, * p1, k1; rep from * to end.

## WOMAN'S VERSION

Rep last 2 rows 9 times more.

## MAN'S VERSION

Rep last 2 rows once more.
*1st buttonhole row*: Rib to last 6 sts, k2, cast off 2, k to end.
*2nd buttonhole row*: K2, cast on 2, k2, rib to end.
Rep rows (1 and 2) 7 times more.

## BOTH VERSIONS

Change to 5½ mm ndls. Keeping the 6 sts at front edge in g-st and remainder in st st beg with a k row, work in patt from chart for left front making buttonholes as before on man's version only as indicated on chart until row 22 of chart has been worked.
Place pocket as follows:
*Next row*: Patt 18/20/22/24, with M p22, patt to end.
*Next row*: Patt 12, with M p22, patt to end.
Rep last 2 rows once more.
*Next row*: Patt 18/20/22/24, with M cast off 22 sts purlwise, patt to end.
*Next row*: Patt 12, then patt across 22 pocket lining sts, patt to end.
Keeping the 6 sts at front edge in g-st and remainder in st st and making buttonholes on man's version only cont in patt from chart until row 82 of chart has been worked.

### Shape raglan armhole

Cont in patt from chart, cast off 7 sts at beg of next row.
Patt 1 row.
Dec 1 st at beg of next row and every foll alt row until 30/32/34/36 sts rem, ending with a right side row.

### Shape neck

Cast off 12 sts at beg of next row.
Complete to match right front from ** to **.

## SLEEVES

With 4½ mm ndls and M yarn, cast on 48/48/50/50 sts using thumb method as shown.
Work 18 rows in k1, p1 rib.
Change to 5½ mm ndls. Work in st st beg with a k row and patt from chart for sleeve beg with 15th/9th/5th/1st row and inc 1 st at both ends of 3rd row and on 0/3/4/8 foll 4th rows, then on every foll 6th row until there are 72/76/80/84 sts.
Cont straight until row 102 of chart has been worked.

### Shape raglan top

Cont in patt from chart, cast off 7 sts at beg of next 2 rows. Dec 1 st at both ends of next row and every foll alt row until 22/26/30/34 sts rem, then at both ends of every row until 4 sts rem.
Cast off.

## COLLAR

With 5½ mm ndls and M yarn, cast on 8 sts.
K 2 rows. Mark end of last row (inside edge) with a coloured thread.
*Next row*: K2, inc in next st, k to last 3 sts, inc in next st, k2.
*Next row*: K.
Rep last 2 rows 4 times more.
*Next row*: K to last 3 sts, inc in next st, k2.
*Next row*: K.
Rep last 2 rows twice more. 21 sts.
Cont straight in g-st until collar measures 39/41/44.5/46 cm (15½/16/17½/18 in) from cast-on edge, ending at inside edge.
*Next row*: K to last 4 sts, k2 tog, k2.
*Next row*: K.
Rep last 2 rows twice more.
*Next row*: K2, k2 tog tbl, k to last 4 sts, k2 tog, k2.
*Next row*: K.
Rep last 2 rows 4 times more. 8 sts.
K 2 rows. Cast off.

# To Make Up

Join raglan, sleeve and side seams using a fine backstitch. Slip stitch cast on edge, inside edge and cast off edge of collar to neck edge, beginning and ending at centre of front bands. Sew pocket linings to wrong side and row ends of pocket tops to right side. Sew buttons to correspond with buttonholes.

KEY

| | | WOMAN'S VERSION | MAN'S VERSION |
|---|---|---|---|
| □ | = M | Winter White | Camel □ |
| ☒ | = A | Sapphire Blue | Navy ☒ |
| ◪ | = B | Spanish Red | Claret ◪ |
| ⊡ | = C | Sunflower Yellow | Cinnamon ⊡ |
| ◩ | = D | Turquoise | Teal ◩ |
| ◪ | = E | Emerald Green | Khaki ◪ |
| ▭ | = 1st Buttonhole Row | | |

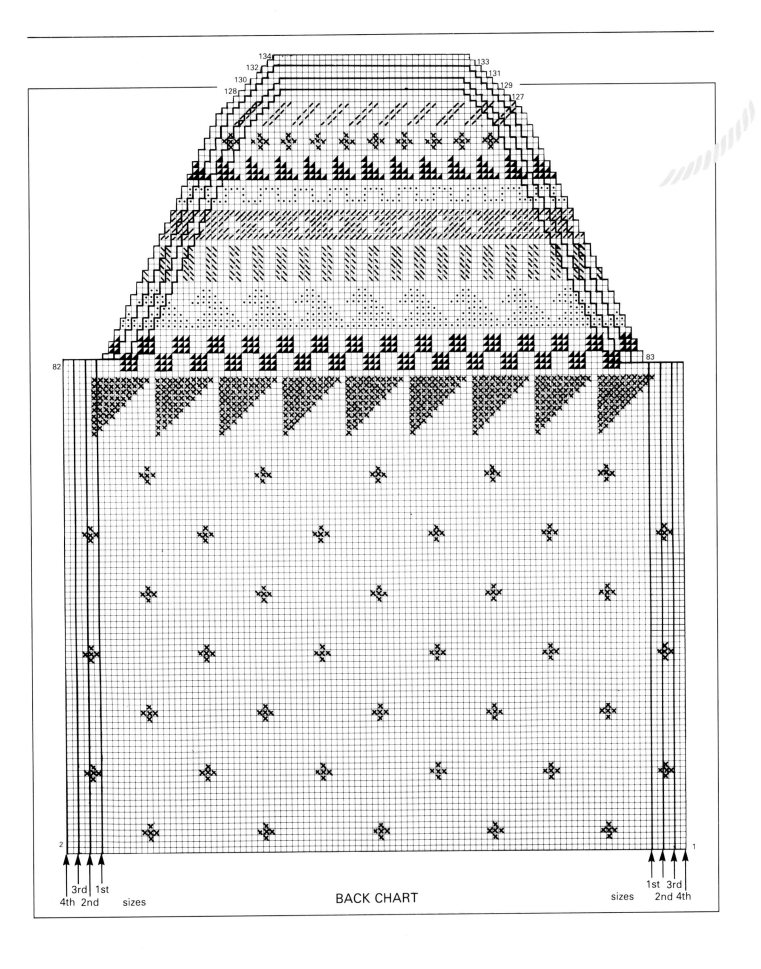

BACK CHART

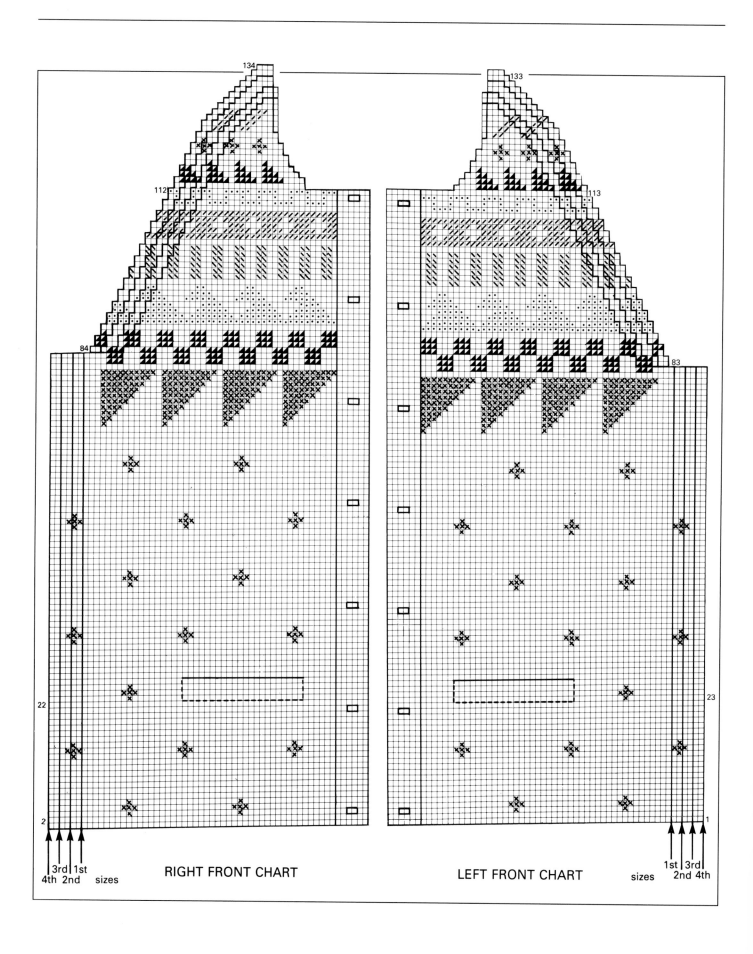

134

133

112

113

84

83

22

23

2

1

3rd 1st
4th 2nd  sizes

**RIGHT FRONT CHART**

**LEFT FRONT CHART**

1st 3rd
sizes  2nd 4th

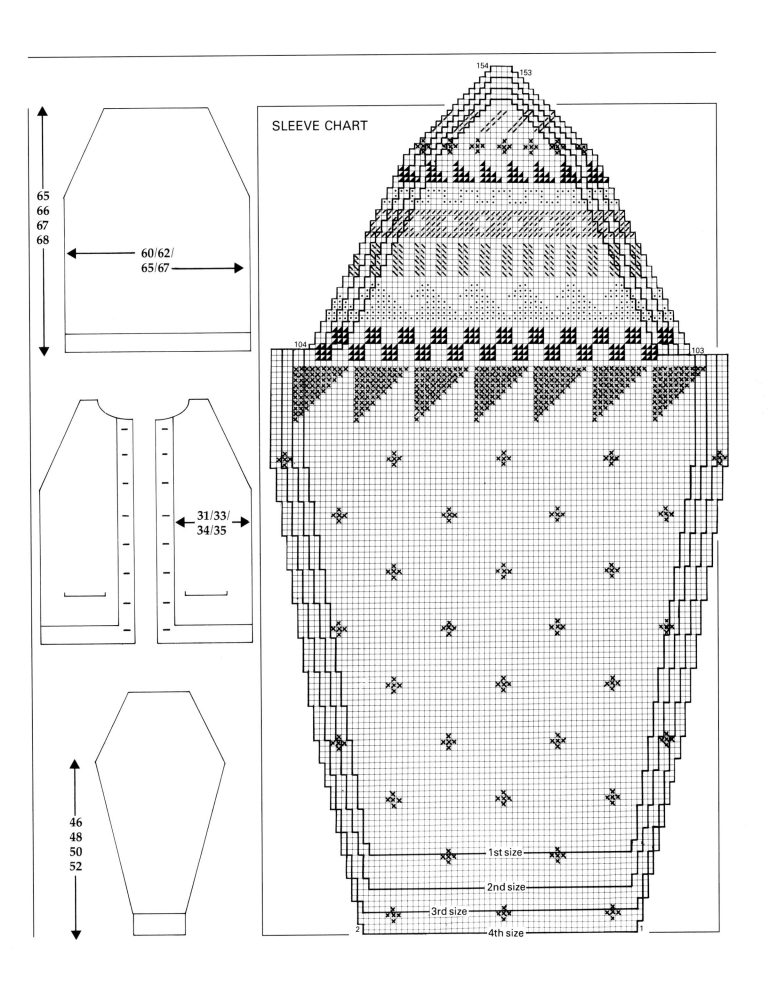

SLEEVE CHART

65
66
67
68

60/62/
65/67

31/33/
34/35

46
48
50
52

154
153
104
103
1st size
2nd size
3rd size
4th size
2
1

MAKE AN EXCITING STATEMENT WITH THIS BRIGHTLY-COLOURED SWEATER

## Stitches used

Mainly in stocking stitch. Welt, cuffs and neckband in one-and-one rib.

## Sizes

Small/medium/large – to suit bust sizes 86/91/97 cm (34/36/38 in); length from shoulder 71 cm (28 in); sleeve seam 46 cm (18 in).

## Materials

Six/six/seven 50g balls Yarnworks Merino Luxury Wool in main shade (801); two/two/two 50g balls each of 820, 818, 822; one/one/one ball each of 821, 805, 806, 817.
The quantities of yarn specified are based on average requirements and are therefore approximate.

## Needles

3¼ mm (no. 10); 4½ mm (no. 7); set of four 3¾ mm (no. 9) double pointed ndls.

## Tension

21 sts and 28 rows to 10 cm (4 in) square measured over st st on 4½ mm ndls.

## Note

Instructions given for three sizes. Use a separate length of yarn for each section and twist yarns together on every row to avoid a hole.

## Instructions

### FRONT

With 3¼ mm ndls and MC, cast on 110/114/118 sts using thumb method. Work 11 cm (4¼ in) k1, p1 rib, inc 6/6/6 sts evenly across last row by working twice into every 18th/19th/19th st. 116/120/124 sts. Change to 4½ mm ndls and st st. Beg with a k row work straight in patt from chart, read odd rows (k) from right to left and even rows (p) from left to right until row 158 of chart is done.

### Shape neck

Next *row*: Patt 42/44/46, turn and leave rem sts on a spare ndl. Dec 1 st at neck edge on next 8 rows. Work 3 rows straight. Cast off. Return to sts on spare ndl. With right side facing, slip first 32 sts on to a holder for neckband, rejoin MC to neck edge and work to correspond with first side.

### BACK

Work exactly as for front to end of row 158 but reverse chart by reading odd rows (k) from left to right and even rows (p) from right to left. Work a further 12 rows straight over all sts in MC to end of row 170. Cast off right across.

### SLEEVES

With 3¼ mm ndls and MC, cast on 54/58/62 sts. Work 6 cm (2½ in) k1, p1 rib.
Change to 4½ mm ndls. Beg with k row, work in st st in patt from chart, shaping sides by inc 1 st at each end of 3rd row, then on every foll 4th row exactly as given on chart 104/108/112 sts, then work straight to end of chart. Cast off right across.
Work a second sleeve the same but reverse chart by reading odd rows (k) from left to right and even rows (p) from right to left.

### NECKBAND

Join shoulder seams. With the set of 3¾ mm ndls and MC, begin at left shoulder seam, pick up and k 12 sts down left side of neck. 32 sts from centre, 12 sts up right side, 48 sts from back of neck. 104 sts. Work 2.5 cm (1 in) in k1, p1 rib, cast off in rib.

## To Make Up

Set in sleeves with centre of sleeve to shoulder seam. Join side and sleeve seams with a fine backstitch.

SLEEVE

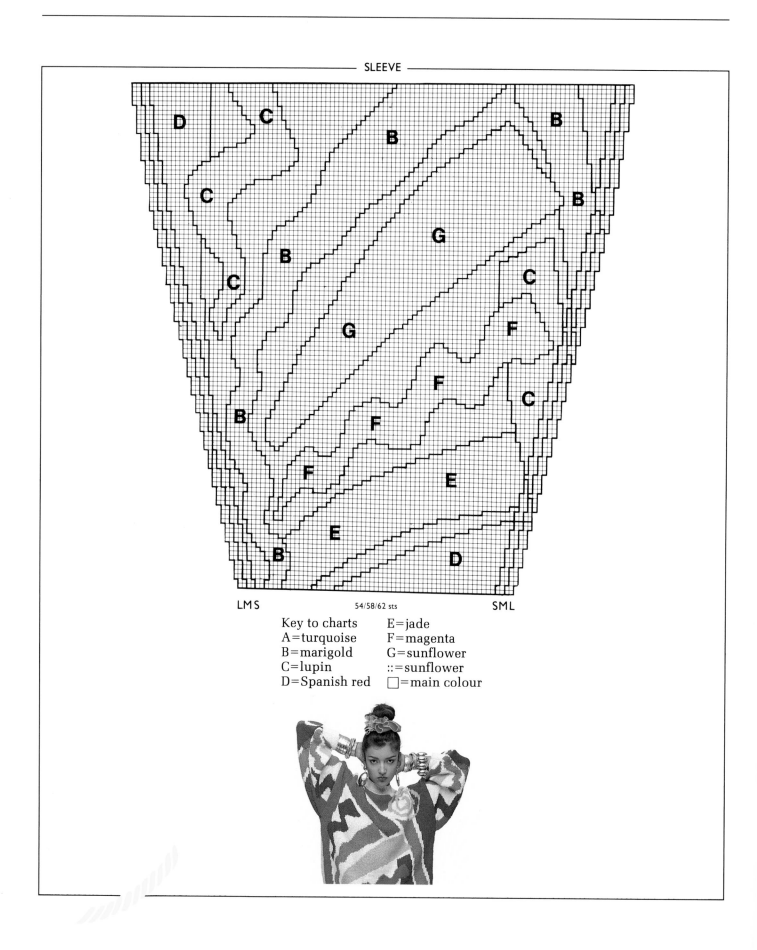

LMS          54/58/62 sts          SML

Key to charts      E=jade
A=turquoise        F=magenta
B=marigold         G=sunflower
C=lupin            ::=sunflower
D=Spanish red      □=main colour

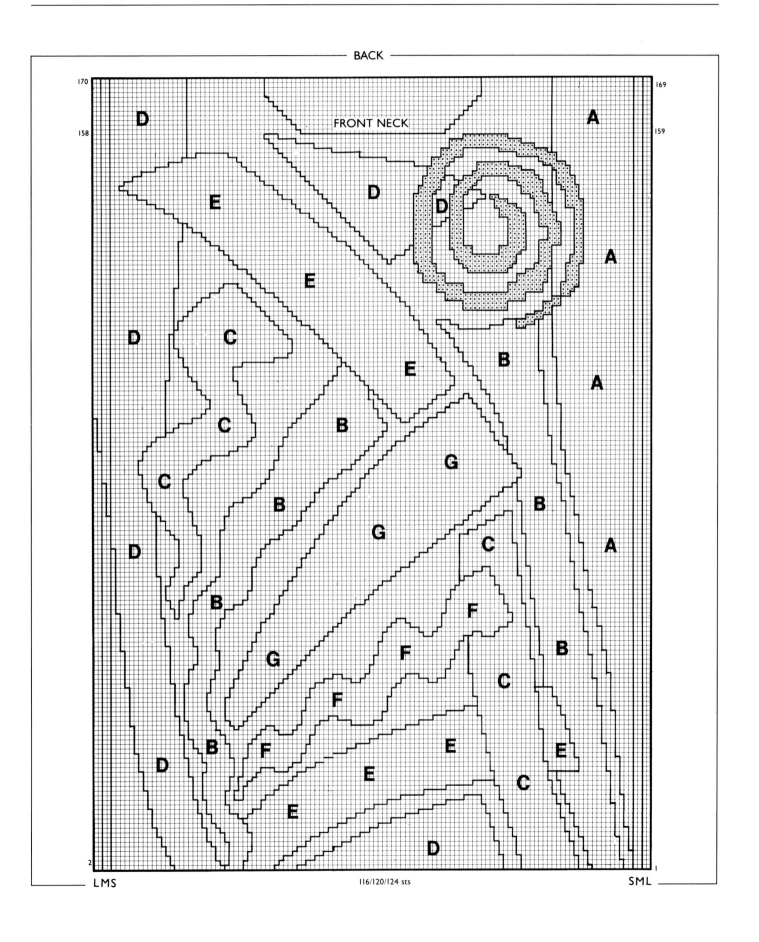

# Catherine Wheel

A CARNIVAL OF COLOUR IN THIS V-FRONTED CARDIGAN

## Stitches used

Mainly in stocking stitch. K1, p1 rib for welts, cuffs and front borders.

## Sizes

Small/medium/large – to suit 86/91/97 cm (34/36/38 in) bust; length from shoulder 71 cm (28 in); sleeve seam 46 cm (18 in).

## Materials

Nine/nine/ten 50g balls of Yarnworks Merino Luxury Wool in main colour 814; two/two/two 50g balls each of five contrasts; 5 buttons.

## Needles

$3\frac{1}{4}$ mm (no. 10); $4\frac{1}{2}$ mm (no. 7).

## Tension

21 sts and 25 rows to 10 cm (4 in) square measured over patt on $4\frac{1}{2}$ mm ndls.

## Note

Do not weave yarns that are not in use. Cut a separate length for each of the motif colours. Twist yarns round each other at back of work when changing colour to avoid a hole. When reading patt from chart, read even numbered rows (p) from left to right and odd numbered rows (k) from right to left.

## Instructions

### BACK

With $3\frac{1}{4}$ mm ndls and MC, cast on 140/146/152 sts. Work 7.5 cm (3 in) k1, p1 rib, dec 20 sts evenly across last row as follows: rib 0/3/6, (rib 5, rib 2 tog) 20 times, rib 0/3/6. (120/126/132 sts).
Change to $4\frac{1}{2}$ mm ndls and st st beg with a k row and work straight in patt from chart until row 154 has been worked. Cast off right across fairly loosely.

### LEFT FRONT

With $3\frac{1}{4}$ mm ndls and MC, cast on 70/73/76 sts. ** Work 7.5 cm (3 in) k1, p1 rib, dec 10 sts evenly across last row: rib 0/2/3, (rib 5, rib 2 tog) 10 times, rib 0/1/3 (60/63/66 sts). ** Change to $4\frac{1}{2}$ mm ndls and st st and work straight in patt from left front chart until row 62 has been worked.

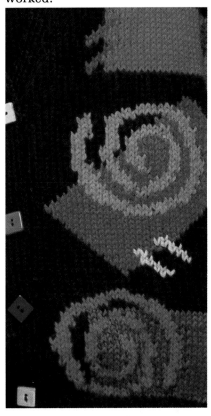

#### Shape front edge

Cont in patt, dec 1 st at end of next row and every foll 4th row as indicated at this edge until 39/42/45 sts remain. Work straight to end of chart (row 154). Cast off.

### RIGHT FRONT

With $3\frac{1}{4}$ mm ndls and MC, cast on 70/73/76 sts and work as for left front from ** to **. Change to $4\frac{1}{2}$ mm ndls and st st and work straight in patt from right front chart, working front shapings as indicated. When row 154 has been worked, cast off.

### SLEEVES

With $3\frac{1}{4}$ mm ndls and MC, cast on 54/60/66 sts. Work 6 cm ($2\frac{1}{2}$ in) in k1, p1 rib.
Change to $4\frac{1}{2}$ mm ndls and st st. Work in patt from chart, shaping sides by inc 1 st at each end of 5th and every foll 4th row until there are 102/108/114 sts. Then at each end of every foll 6th row until there are 106/112/118 sts. Work straight to end of chart. Cast off right across.

### FRONT BORDERS

Join shoulder seams on wrong side with fine backstitch.
*Left*: With $3\frac{1}{4}$ mm ndls and MC, cast on 7 sts. Work in k1, p1 rib until strip is long enough to go up left front and round to centre back of neck when slightly stretched. Sew in place on wrong side with flat seam.
*Right*: Work a similar piece for right front with the addition of 5 buttonholes – first to come 1 cm ($\frac{1}{2}$ in) from lower edge, 5th one 2 cm ($\frac{3}{4}$ in) below start of front shaping and remainder spaced evenly between. Mark position of buttons on left front with pins – work buttonholes to correspond. To make a buttonhole, rib 3, cast off 2, rib 2, turn, rib 2, cast on 2, rib 3.

## To Make Up

Pin cast-off edge of sleeves into armholes centre of sleeve top to come at shoulder seam; join with fine backstitch; join rest of side and sleeve seams. Join rib at back of neck. Sew on buttons.

BACK

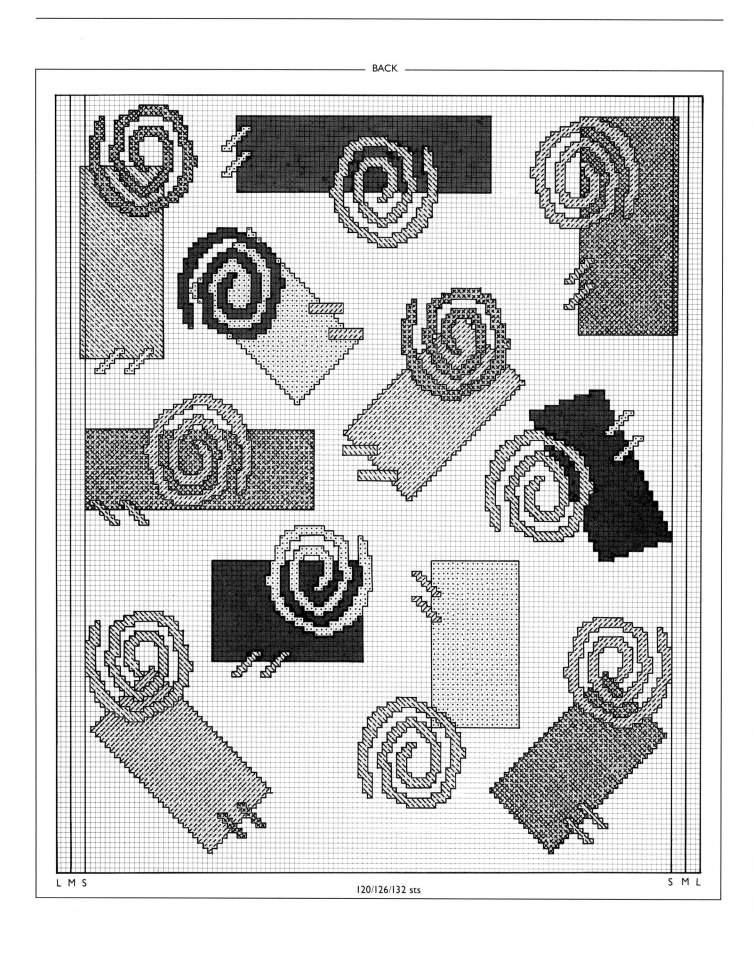

L M S

120/126/132 sts

S M L

RIGHT FRONT

LEFT FRONT

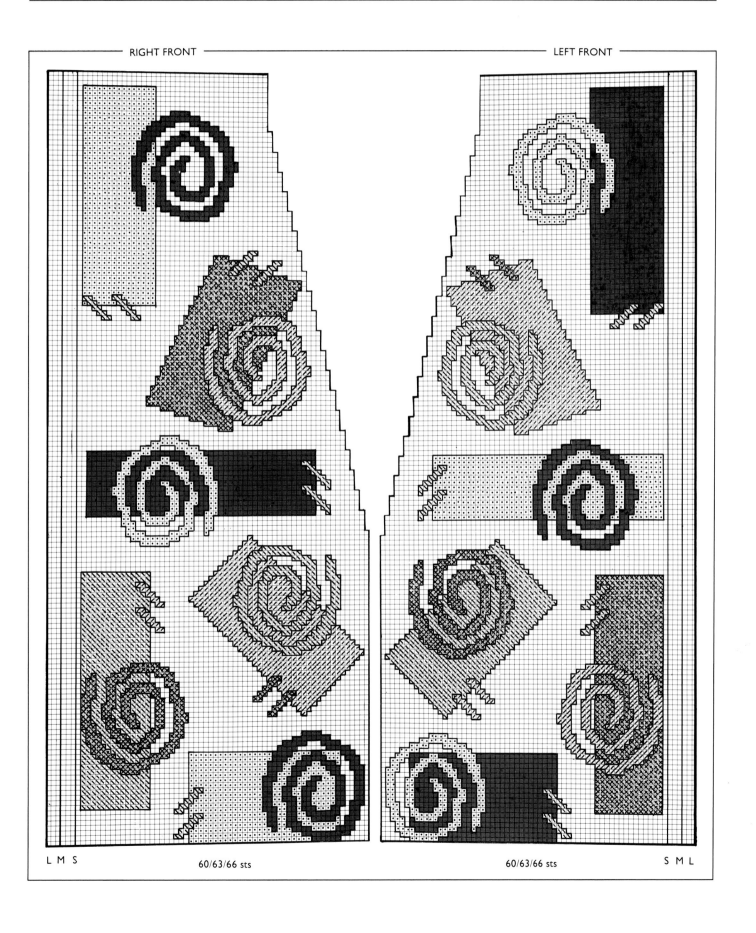

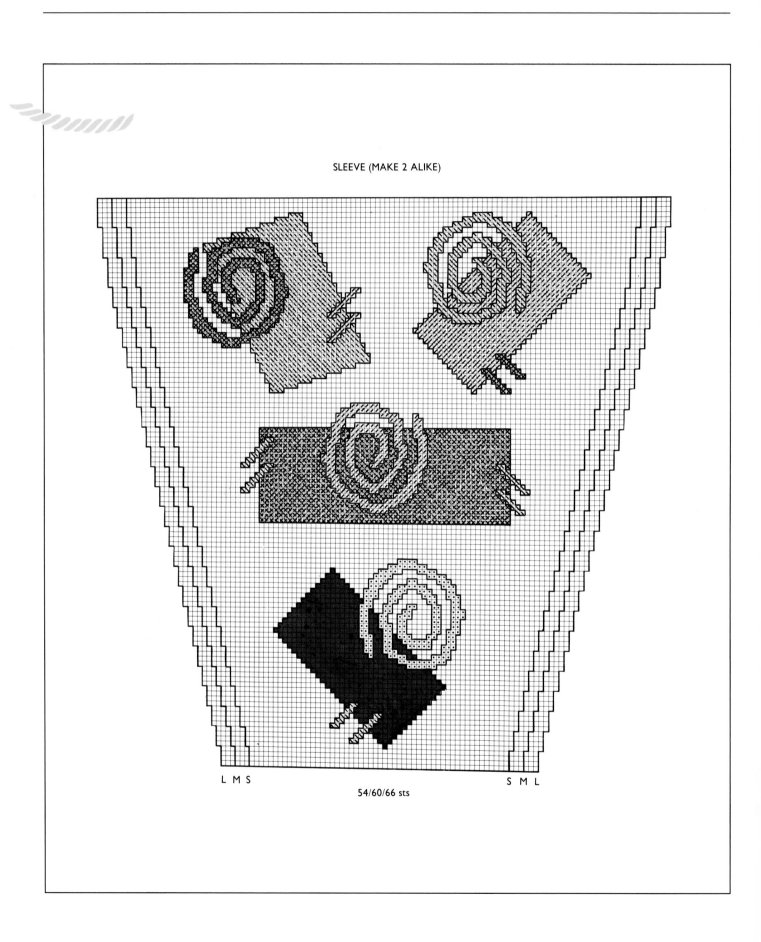

SLEEVE (MAKE 2 ALIKE)

L M S                                    S M L

54/60/66 sts

# Over the Moon

A FUN CHILDREN'S CARDIGAN OR SWEATER WITH NAVY OR WHITE BACKGROUND

## Stitches used

Mainly in stocking stitch and multi-colour pattern. Welts, cuffs, neckband or front bands in one-and-one rib.

## Sizes

1st size/2nd size/3rd size to suit chest sizes 61/67/71 cm (24/26/28 in); length 35/40/45 cm (14/16/18 in); sleeve seam 26/31/34 cm (10¼/12¼/13½ in).

## Materials

Four/four/five 50g balls of main colour in Yarnworks Merino Luxury Wool, and one 50g ball of same yarn in each of five contrast colours for both versions; 5 buttons for cardigan. The quantities of yarn specified are based on average requirements and are therefore approximate.

## Needles

3¼ mm (no. 10); 4½ mm (no. 7); 4 st-holders for sweater.

## Tension

20 sts and 28 rows to 10 cm (4 in) square measured over stocking stitch on 4½ mm ndls.

## Note

Use a separate ball of yarn for each colour area and twist yarns together on wrong side to avoid a hole. When working from chart, read odd-numbered (K) rows from right to left and even-numbered (P) rows from left to right. Instructions given for three sizes.

## Special abbreviations

A – 1st contrast; B – 2nd contrast; C – 3rd contrast; D – 4th contrast; E – 5th contrast; M – Main colour.

## Instructions

### SWEATER BACK

With 3¼ mm ndls and M cast on 70/76/80 sts using thumb method.
Work in k1, p1 rib for 4/4/5 cm (1½/1½/2 in).
Change to 4½ mm ndls. Work in st st beg with a k row and patt from back chart, beg with row 21/11/1 until row 66 of chart has been worked.

### Shape raglan armholes

Cont in patt from chart, cast off 1/2/3 sts at beg of next 2 rows. ** Dec 1 st at both ends of next row and every foll alt row until 26/28/28 sts rem, ending with a p row. Sl these sts on to a st-holder.

### FRONT

Work as given for back to ** but work patt from front chart. Dec 1 st at both ends of next row and every foll alt row until 36/38/38 sts rem, ending with a p row.

### Shape neck

Next row: Work 2 tog, patt 12, turn; leave the rem sts on a spare ndl. Cont on first set of sts for left half front. Cont to dec at raglan edge on every foll alt row at the same time, dec 1 st at neck edge on next row and 2 foll alt rows then on every row until 2 sts rem. K2 tog and fasten off.

With right side of work facing, sl first 8/10/10 sts from spare ndl on to a st-holder and leave for centre front neck, rejoin M yarn to rem sts and patt to last 2 sts, work 2 tog. Complete right half front to match left half front.

### SLEEVES

With 3¼ mm ndls and M cast on 37/39/41 sts.
Row 1 (right side): K1, * p1, k1; rep from * to end.
Row 2: P1, * k1, p1; rep from * to end.
Rep these 2 rows until rib measures 5 cm (2 in) from cast-on edge, ending with row 2.
Change to 4½ mm ndls.
Work in st st beg with a k row and patt from sleeve chart. Beg with row 25/11/1 and inc 1 st at both ends of 3rd row and 6 foll 4th rows then on every foll 3rd/4th/5th row until there are 69/73/75 sts. Patt 4/5/5 rows straight. *****

### Shape raglan top

Cont in patt from chart, cast off 1/2/3 sts at beg of next 2 rows. Dec 1 st at both ends of next row and every foll alt row until 33/33/29 sts rem then at both ends of every row until 15 sts rem. Sl these sts on to a st-holder.

### NECKBAND

Join raglan seams using a fine backstitch, leaving left back seam open.
With M yarn, 3¼ mm ndls and right side of work facing k the 15 sts from st-holder on top of left sleeve, pick up and k 10 sts from shaped edge of left front neck, k the 8/10/10 sts from st-holder at centre front neck, pick up and k 10 sts from shaped edge of right front neck, k the 15 sts from st-holder on top of right sleeve then k the 26/28/28 sts from st-holder at centre back neck. 84/88/88 sts.
Work 2 cm (¾ in) in k1, p1 rib. Cast off in rib.

# To Make Up

Join left back raglan and neckband seam using a fine backstitch. Join side and sleeve seams.

## CARDIGAN
### BACK

Work as given for back of sweater, but cast off sts at centre back neck.

### LEFT FRONT

With 3¼ mm ndls and M cast on 34/38/40 sts. Work in k1, p1 rib for 4/4/5 cm (1½/1½/2 in) and inc 1 st at centre of last row on first size only. 35/38/40 sts.
Change to 4½ mm ndls.
Work in st st, beg with a k row and patt from left front chart beg with row 21/11/1 until row 50 of chart has been worked ***.
Cont in patt from chart dec 1 st at end of next row and 2 foll 6th rows. Patt 3 rows straight.

**Shape raglan armhole**
Cont in patt from chart, cast off 1/2/3 sts at beg of next row. Patt 1 row. **** Cont to dec at front edge on next row and 4 foll 6th rows then on 3/4/4 foll 4th rows at the same time dec 1 st at raglan edge on next row and every foll alt row until 4/3/4 sts rem. Keeping front edge straight cont to dec at raglan edge on 2/1/2 foll alt rows. Work 1 row. K2 tog and fasten off.

### RIGHT FRONT

Work as given for left front to *** but work patt from right front chart. Cont in patt from chart, dec 1 st at beg of next row and 2 foll 6th rows. Patt 4 rows straight.

**Shape raglan armhole**
Cont in patt from chart, cast off 1/2/3 sts at beg of next row.
Complete to match left front from **** to end.

### SLEEVES

Work as given for sleeves of sweater to *****.

**Shape raglan top**
Cont in patt from chart, cast off 1/2/3 sts at beg of next 2 rows. Dec 1 st at both ends of next row and every foll alt row until 43/43/39 sts rem then at both ends of every row until 5 sts rem. Cast off.

### BUTTON BAND

Join raglan seams using a fine backstitch.
With 3¼ mm ndls and M cast on 7 sts. Work in rib as given for sleeves of sweater until band when slightly stretched will fit along front edge to centre back neck.
Cast off in rib. Sew buttonband neatly to left front for girl or right front for boy. Mark band with pins to indicate buttons, first one to be 1 cm (¼ in) up from cast-on edge and last one at beg of front shaping, rem 3 spaced evenly between.

### BUTTONHOLE BAND

Work buttonhole band to match button band, making buttonholes at pin positions as follows:
*1st buttonhole row*: Rib 3, cast off 2, rib to end.
*2nd buttonhole row*: Work in rib casting on 2 sts over those cast off to complete buttonhole.

# To Make Up

Sew buttonhole band neatly into position, then join cast off edges. Join side and sleeve seams using a fine backstitch. Sew on buttons to correspond with buttonholes.

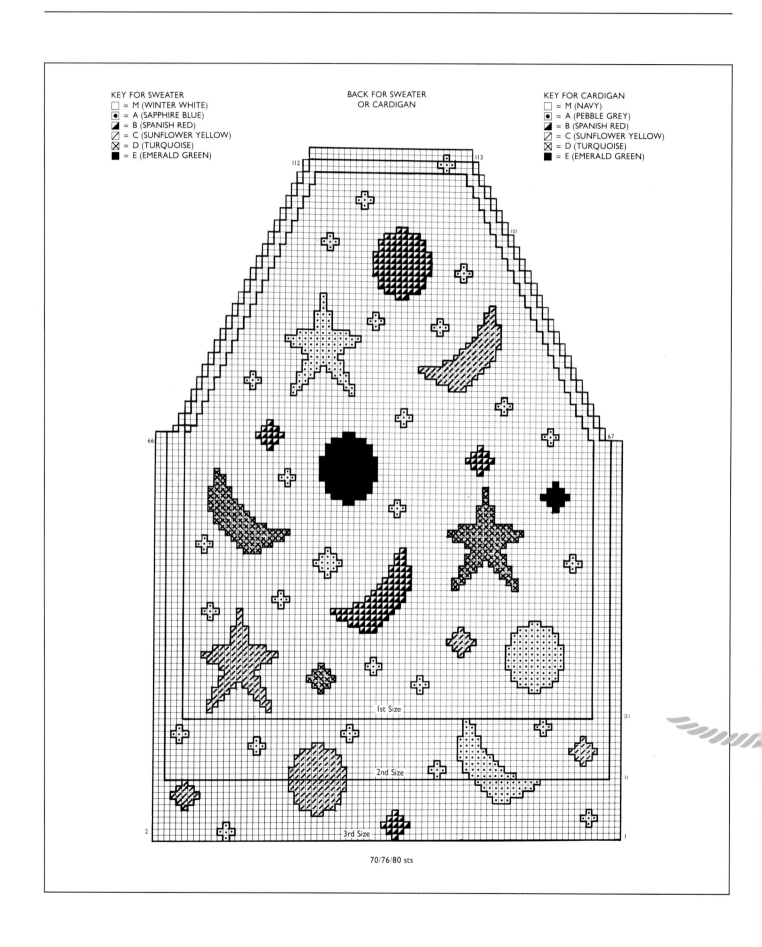

KEY FOR SWEATER
☐ = M (WINTER WHITE)
⊡ = A (SAPPHIRE BLUE)
◩ = B (SPANISH RED)
◪ = C (SUNFLOWER YELLOW)
⊠ = D (TURQUOISE)
■ = E (EMERALD GREEN)

BACK FOR SWEATER
OR CARDIGAN

KEY FOR CARDIGAN
☐ = M (NAVY)
⊡ = A (PEBBLE GREY)
◩ = B (SPANISH RED)
◪ = C (SUNFLOWER YELLOW)
⊠ = D (TURQUOISE)
■ = E (EMERALD GREEN)

1st Size

2nd Size

3rd Size

70/76/80 sts

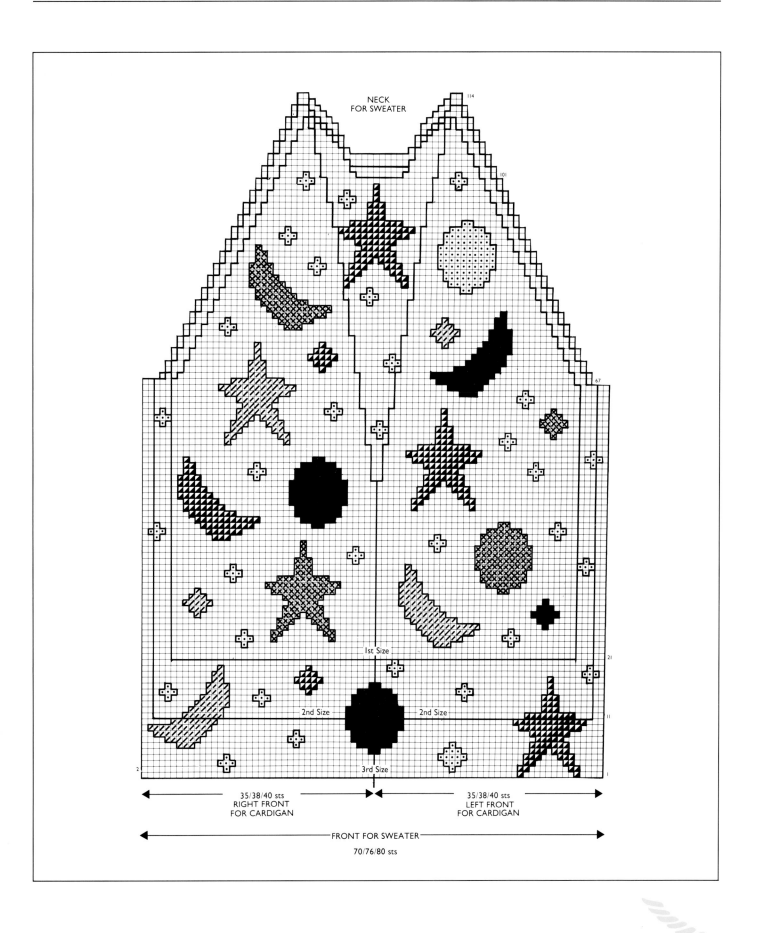

NECK
FOR SWEATER

114

101

67

1st Size

21

2nd Size | 2nd Size

11

3rd Size

2

35/38/40 sts
RIGHT FRONT
FOR CARDIGAN

35/38/40 sts
LEFT FRONT
FOR CARDIGAN

FRONT FOR SWEATER
70/76/80 sts

SLEEVE

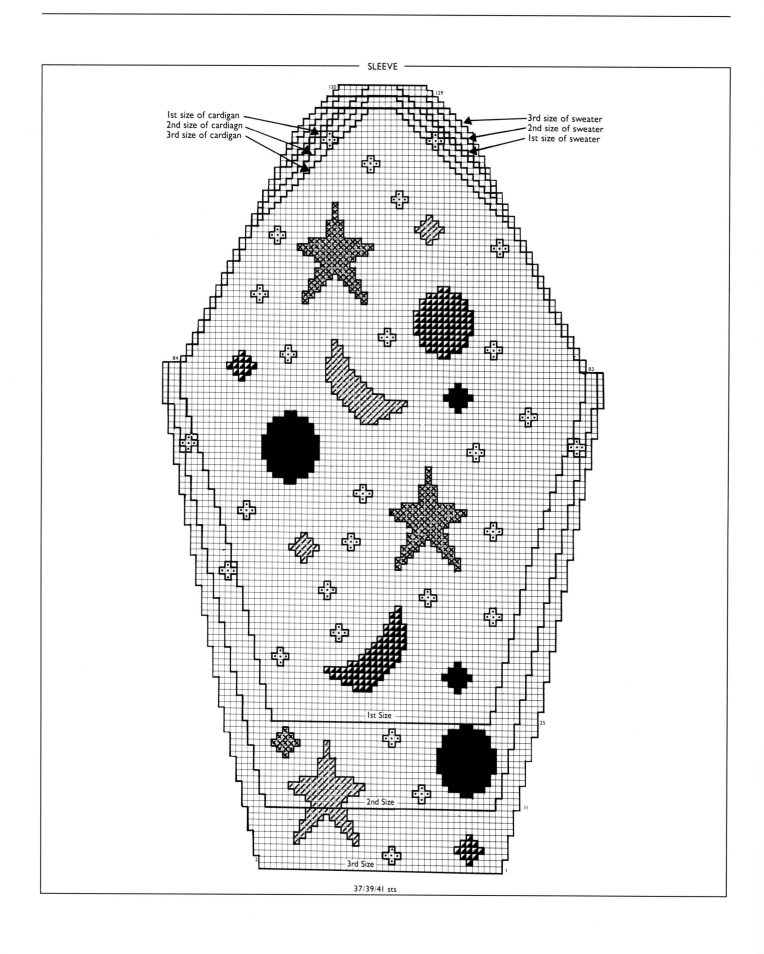

1st size of cardigan
2nd size of cardiagn
3rd size of cardigan

3rd size of sweater
2nd size of sweater
1st size of sweater

130

129

84

83

1st Size

25

2nd Size

11

3rd Size

2

1

37/39/41 sts

# Snakes and Ladders

ORIGINAL COLLARED SWEATER FOR BOYS AND GIRLS

## Stitches used
Mainly in panels of cable and stocking stitch. One-and-one rib for welts, cuffs and collar.

## Sizes
Small/medium/large – to suit chest sizes 61/66/71 cm (24/26/28 in); length from shoulder about 38/43/48 cm (15/17/19 in); sleeve seam 26.5/30.5/34 cm (10½/12/13½ in).

## Materials
Nine/nine/ten 50g balls of Yarn-works Merino Luxury Wool of which two/two/three balls are winter white, two/two/three balls pebble grey; one/one/one ball each of Spanish red, emerald, sapphire, sunflower and turquoise.
The quantities of yarn specified are based on average requirements and are therefore approximate.

## Needles
3¼ mm (no. 10); 4½ mm (no. 7); set of four double-pointed 3¾ (no. 9) ndls for neckband and collar; cable needle; st-holder.

## Tension
20 sts and 30 rows to 10 cm (4 in) square measured over pattern on 4½ mm ndls.

## Note
Instructions given for three sizes.

## Special abbreviations
C8F – Cable 8 front (slip next 4 sts on to a cable needle and leave at front of work, k next 4 sts, then k the 4 sts from cable needle). W – winter white; G – grey.

## Instructions

### BACK

With 3¼ mm ndls and sunflower cast on 70/76/82 sts.
Work in k1, p1 rib for 5 cm (2 in).
*Inc row:* Rib 10/11/12, * (inc into next st) twice, rib 9/6/5; rep from * ending last rep with rib 14/15/12. 80/90/100 sts.
Change to 4½ mm ndls and work in patt as follows:

*Row 1* (right side): With W k10/13/16, with emerald k8, with W k5/6/7, with sapphire k8, with W k5/6/7, with sunflower k8, with W k5/6/7, with Spanish red k8, with W k5/6/7, with turquoise k8, with W k10/13/16.
*Row 2:* Keeping colours as now set and twisting the yarns when changing colour to avoid a hole, purl.
*Row 3:* As row 1, but use G instead of W.
*Row 4:* As row 2, but use G instead of W.
*Row 5:* With W k10/13/16, with emerald C8F – see special abbreviations – with W k5/6/7, with sapphire C8F, with W k5/6/7, with sunflower C8F, with W k5/6/7, with Spanish red C8F, with W k5/6/7, with turquoise C8F, with W k10/13/16.
*Row 6:* As row 2.
*Row 7:* As row 3.
*Row 8:* As row 4.
These 8 rows form the patt. Rep them until 7/8/10 cable rows in all have been worked. Patt 1/5/1 rows.

### Shape raglan
Keeping patt correct cast off 3 sts at beg of next 2 rows, then dec 1 st at each end of next row and every foll alt row until 60/64/68 sts rem (the 8 sts of emerald and turquoise cables are at each end of work).
Now dec 1 st at each end of next 5 rows. 50/54/58 sts. ***
Now dec 1 st at each end of next row and every foll alt row until 32/34/36 sts rem.
*Next row* (wrong side): P1, (p2 tog) twice, patt to last 5 sts, (p2 tog) twice, p1.
*Next row:* K2 tog, patt to last 2 sts, k2 tog tb1.
*Next row:* P2 tog tbl, patt 9/10/11, (p2 tog) twice, patt to last 2 sts, p2 tog.
Leave rem 22/24/26 sts on a spare ndl.

### FRONT

Work as given for back to ***, then cont as follows:
Dec 1 st at each end of next row and foll 1/2/3 alt rows. 46/48/50 sts.
*Next row* (wrong side): Patt 21/22/23 sts, (p2 tog) twice, patt to end.

### Shape neck
*Next row:* K2 tog, patt 15/16/17 sts, turn; leaving rem 27/28/29 sts on a spare ndl. Cont on first set of 16/17/18 sts thus:
*Row 1:* P2 tog tbl, patt to end.
*Row 2:* K2 tog, patt to last 2 sts, k2 tog tb1.
Rep rows 1 and 2 once more. 10/11/12 sts.

*Next row*: P1/2/3, (p2 tog) twice, p5.

*Next row*: K2 tog, patt to last 2 sts, k2 tog tbl.

*Next row*: Work in patt without dec.

Dec 1 st at beg of next row and every foll alt row until all sts have been worked off.

Fasten off.

Return to rem 27/28/29 sts left on spare ndl, sl centre 10 sts on to st-holder and with right side of work facing rejoin yarn to neck edge and work as follows:

*Row 1*: Patt to last 2 sts, k2 tog tbl.

*Row 2*: Patt to last 2 sts, p2 tog.

*Row 3*: K2 tog, patt to last 2 sts, k2 tog tbl.

Rep rows 2 and 3 once more. 10/11/12 sts.

Complete to match first side, reversing all shaping.

### RIGHT SLEEVE

With 3¼ mm ndls and sunflower cast on 38/40/42 sts. Work in k1, p1 rib for 4 cm (1½ in).

*Inc row*: Rib 5/4/3, *(inc in next st) twice, rib 9/10/11; rep from * to end. 44/46/48 sts.

Change to 4½ mm ndls and work in patt as follows:

*Row 1*: With W k5, with turquoise k8, with W k5/6/7, with sapphire k8, with W k5/6/7, with emerald k8, with W k5.

Keeping the colours as now set for cable panels and working the st st panels in stripes of W/G as for back cont in patt and work 5 rows more, then inc 1 st at each end of next row and every foll 6th row until there are 54/58/62 sts, working the

extra sts into W/G stripe patt as they are made.

Cont straight in patt until 8/10/11 cable rows have been worked altogether.

Patt 5/1/5 rows.

### Shape raglan

Cast off 3 sts at beg of next 2 rows, then dec 1 st at each end of next row and every foll alt row until 34/36/38 sts rem, then dec 1 st at each end of next 5 rows, after which dec 1 st at each end of next row and every foll alt row until 4 sts rem, omitting the last centre cable twist on small and large sizes. Purl one row. Leave these sts on a spare ndl.

### LEFT SLEEVE

Work as given for right sleeve, but work the cable colours as follows:

*Row 1*: With W k5, with turquoise k8, with W k5/6/7, with Spanish red k8, with W k5/6/7, with emerald k8, with W k5.

### NECKBAND AND COLLAR

Join turquoise yarn at right side of the 10 centre front sts, then with set of four 3¾ mm ndls and right side of work facing k the 10 centre front sts from st-holder, then pick up and k18/20/22 sts from right front neck edge, k across the 4 sts at top of sleeve, k across the 22/24/26 sts from back neck, then the 4 sts at top of sleeve and finally pick up and k18/20/22 sts from left front neck edge. 76/82/88 sts.

Working in rounds work 3 rounds in k1, p1 rib. Break off turquoise yarn. Slip next 5 sts, turn, so that wrong side is facing at centre front of neck.

Join in Spanish red yarn, inc in first st, rib 23/25/27 sts more, join in emerald yarn, rib 27/29/31 sts, join in sapphire yarn, rib 25/27/29 sts, turn.

Working in rows, keeping the three colours as now set and twisting the colours at right side of garment (wrong side of collar), work 14 rows in k1, p1 rib.

Cast off loosely in rib, changing colour one st early.

## To Make Up

Do not press. Set in sleeves, then join sleeve and side seams, using a fine backstitch.

# Maypole

## Stitches used
Mainly in stocking stitch. One-and-one rib for welts and cuffs, graded rib for yoke.

## Sizes
Small/medium – to suit bust 86/91 cm (34/36 in); length from cast-off edge at centre back of neck to cast-on edge about 66.5 cm (26¼ in); sleeve seam about 41 cm (16 in).

## Materials
Ten/eleven 50g balls of Yarnworks Merino Luxury Wool in main colour (black) and one/one 50g ball in each of the following contrast colours: emerald, lupin, turquoise, sunflower (yellow), magenta, Spanish red, sapphire.
The quantities of yarn specified are based on average requirements and are therefore approximate.

## Needles
3¼ mm (no. 10); 4½ mm (no. 7); 3¾ mm (no. 9) circular ndl for yoke; st-holder.

## Tension
22 sts and 28 rows to 10 cm (4 in) square measured over stocking stitch on 4½ mm ndls.

## Note
Instructions given for two sizes.

## Special abbreviations
M1k – make 1 knit (by picking up loop that lies between st just worked and following st and k into the back of it); M1p – make 1 purl (as M1k but purl into back of loop). MC – main colour; C – contrast; E – emerald; T – turquoise; M – magenta; S – sapphire; L – lupin; Y – yellow (Sunflower); R – Spanish red.

## Instructions

### Note
The sts used in the raindrop shapes are increased at the beg and decreased at the end of each shape and are not included in the basic number of sts given. Twist yarns round each other at back of work when changing colour to avoid a hole. Use short lengths or small balls of contrast for each raindrop.

### RAINDROP PATTERN

Raindrop patt over 2 sts of contrast when started on odd-numbered rows on chart are worked as follows:
*Row 1*: With C M1k.
*Row 2*: P into back and front of contrast st.
*Row 3*: K2 in contrast.
*Row 4*: P2 in contrast.
*Rows 5 and 6*: As rows 3 and 4.
*Row 7*: Sl the st before the 2 contrast sts, k2 tog the 2 contrast sts in MC, then pass slipped st over.
Raindrop pattern over 2 sts of contrast when started on even-numbered rows on chart are worked as follows:
*Row 1*: With C M1p.
*Row 2*: K into back and front of contrast st.
*Row 3*: P2 in contrast.
*Row 4*: K2 in contrast.
*Rows 5 and 6*: As rows 3 and 4.
*Row 7*: Sl the st before the 2 contrast sts, p tog the 2 contrast sts in MC, then pass slipped st over.

### BACK

With 3¼ mm ndls and MC cast on 101/107 sts.
*Row 1*: K1, * p1, k1; rep from * to end.
*Row 2*: P1, * k1, p1; rep from * to end.
Rep last 2 rows for 7.5 cm (3 in), ending with a row 1.
*Inc row* (wrong side): P2/8, * inc into next st, p10/10; rep from * to end. 110/116 sts.

Change to 4½ mm ndls. **
Now work in raindrop patt from chart – the heavy line indicates the position of each raindrop and the 7 rows over which it is worked, use the colours as indicated beside the heavy lines, joining in and breaking off the colours as required. As the sts are extra to the basic number of sts they are not shown on the chart. The background is worked in st st in MC. Read chart from right to left on odd-numbered rows (k rows) and from left to right on even-numbered rows (p rows). Work to end of row 82 – work should now measure about 38 cm (15 in) from cast-on edge.

### Shape raglan
Cast off 3/6 sts at beg of next 2 rows, then dec 1 st at each end of next row and every foll alt row as shown on chart until 80/80 sts rem. P one row – work should now measure about 48.5 cm (19 in) from cast-on edge. Leave sts on a spare ndl until required for yoke.

### FRONT

Work as given for back to **, then follow chart given for front.
Work to end of row 92.
Divide sts for neck as indicated on chart, leaving centre 44 sts on a st-holder until required for yoke.

### SLEEVES (both alike)

With 3¼ mm ndls and MC cast on 44/46 sts. Work 7.5 cm (3 in) in k1, p1 rib.
*Inc row*: Purl and inc 10/10 sts evenly across row. 54/56 sts.
Change to 4½ mm ndls and work from chart given for sleeves, shaping as shown on chart until there are 80/82 sts.
Work straight to end of row 92 – work should now measure about 41 cm (16 in) from cast-on edge.
Shape raglan top as shown on chart. Leave rem 56/56 sts on a spare ndl.

## YOKE

With right side of work facing and circular 3¾ mm ndl and MC work as follows:
Divide the 44 sts left on st-holder at centre front neck between two ndls (that is 22 sts on one ndl and 22 sts on 2nd ndl), begin at centre front sts and k22 sts from 1st ndl, then pick up and k17 sts up right front neck edge, k56 sts from top of right sleeve, k80 sts from back neck edge, k56 sts from top of left sleeve, pick up and k17 sts down left front neck edge, then k across the 22 sts from 2nd ndl at centre front. (270 sts).

Now work in rounds of striped rib as follows:
*Round 1*: K1 R, (p4 MC, k1 MC) twice, p4 MC, k1 S, (p4 MC, k1 MC) twice, p4 MC, k1 M, (p4 MC, k1 MC) twice, p4 MC, k1 L, (p4 MC, k1 MC) twice, p4 MC, k1 T, (p4 MC, k1 MC) twice, p4 MC, k1 Y, (p4 MC, k1 MC) twice, p4 MC, k1 E, (p4 MC, k1 MC) twice, p4 MC, k1 R, (p4 MC, k1 MC) twice, p4 MC, k1 T, (p4 MC, k1 MC) twice, p4 MC, k1 L, (p4 MC, k1 MC) twice, p4 MC, k1 M, (p4 MC, k1 MC) twice, p4 MC, k1 Y, (p4 MC, k1 MC) twice, p4 MC, k1 T, (p4 MC, k1 MC) twice, p4 MC, k1

BACK

80 sts

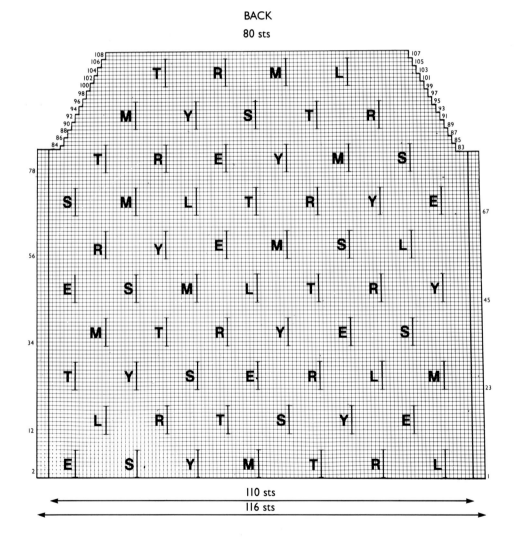

110 sts

116 sts

R, (p4 MC, k1 MC) twice, p4 MC, k1 S, (p4 MC, k1 MC) twice, p4 MC, k1 E, (p4 MC, k1 MC) twice, p4 MC, k1 Y, (p4 MC, k1 MC) twice, p4 MC, k1 T, (p4 MC, k1 MC) twice, p4 MC. (This round sets the 18 contrast ribs.)

Cont in colours as now set thus:

*Round 2* (inc round): * Inc into next st with C, (p4 MC, k1 MC) twice, p4 MC; rep from * all round. (288 sts.)

*Round 3*: * K2 C, (p4 MC, k1 MC) twice, p4 MC; rep from * all round. Rep round 3 eight times more.

*Round 12*: * K2 C, (p2 MC, p2 tog MC, k1 MC) twice, p2 MC, p2 tog MC; rep from * all round. (234 sts.)
Work 12 rounds straight as now set.

*Round 25*: * K2 C, (p1 MC, p2 tog MC, k1 MC) twice, p1 MC, p2 tog MC; rep from * all round. (180 sts.)
Work 12 rounds straight as now

set.

*Round 38*: * K2 C, (p2 tog MC, k1 MC) twice, p2 tog MC; rep from * all round. (126 sts.)
Work 10 rounds straight as now set.

*Round 49*: * K2 C, p1 MC, k2 tog MC, k1 MC, ·p1 MC rep from * all round. (108 sts.)
Work 8 rounds straight as now set.
Cast off loosely in rib using the appropriate colours.

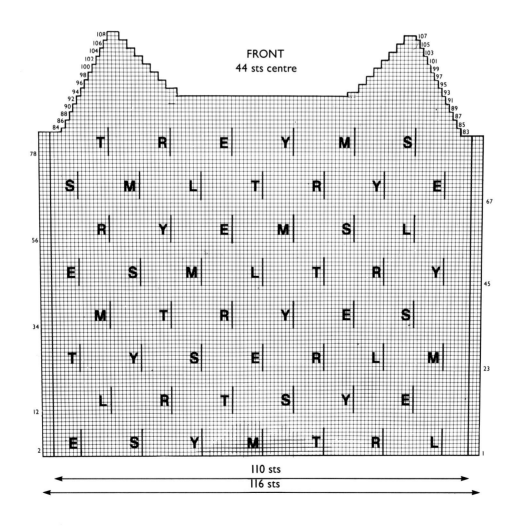

FRONT
44 sts centre

110 sts

116 sts

## SLEEVE
### 56 sts

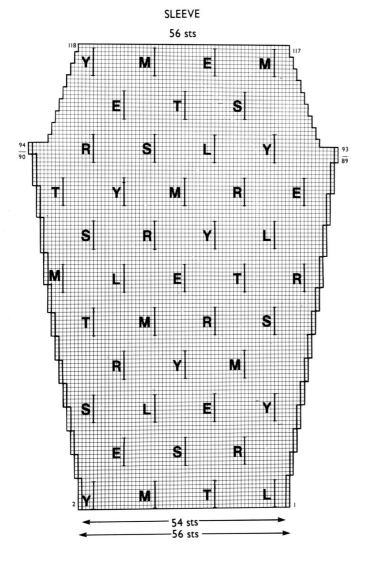

*To Make Up*

Do not press. Set in raglan sleeves, using a flat seam. Join sleeve and side seams, using a fine backstitch. Tighten ends of coloured yarns at top and base of each raindrop to get a good shape, then darn in ends.

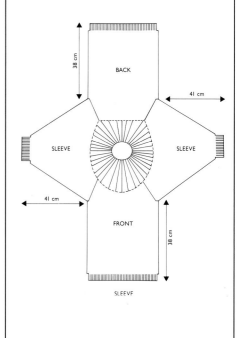

# Hourglass

## Stitches used
Mainly in stocking stitch and reversed stocking stitch. One-and-one rib for cuffs.

## Sizes
Medium – to suit bust size 91 cm (36 in); length from shoulder to lower edge 60 cm (23½ in); sleeve seam 43 cm (17 in).

## Materials
Eleven 50g balls of Yarnworks Merino Luxury Wool.
The quantities of yarn specified are based on average requirements and are therefore approximate.

## Needles
3¾ mm (no. 9) and 4½ mm (no. 7); a 4½ mm (no. 7) circular ndl to accommodate large number of sts when necessary; stitch-holders.

## Tension
22 sts and 28 rows to 10 cm (4 in) square measured over stocking stitch on 4½ mm ndls.

## Note
It is very important that you check your tension carefully before you begin this design. The tension of the knitting controls the size of the finished garment. If your sample has less sts than our tension, try again with smaller ndls and vice versa, then work the garment with the ndls which produce our tension.

This sweater is knitted sideways in one piece, starting at wrist edge of left sleeve and working across to wrist edge of right sleeve.

There are two different ridge patterns. Ridge pattern one is used at lower edge of back and front. Ridge pattern two is used at centre of sleeves and for yoke and has two extra turning rows to give more elasticity across the yoke. *These two turning rows are not indicated on the chart.*

Ridge pattern one is worked as follows:
*Row 1* (right side): P.
*Row 2*: K.

*Row 3*: K.
*Row 4*: P.
These 4 rows form ridge pattern one.
Ridge pattern two is worked as follows:
*Row 1* (right side): P.
*Row 2*: K.
*Row 3*: K.

*Row 4*: P.
*Row 5*: P.
*Row 6*: K.
*Row 7*: K the ridge patt sts, turn.
*Row 8*: P the ridge patt sts, turn.
*Row 9*: P the ridge patt sts.
*Row 10*: K.
*Row 11*: K.
*Row 12*: P.

These 12 rows set the ridge pattern two.

Ridge pattern two will have st st at each side. This will separate ridge pattern two from ridge pattern one at lower edge of the back and front as indicated on chart. The chart also shows the side and sleeve increasings and the shaping of ridge patterns.

## Instructions

Begin at cuff edge of left sleeve by casting on 48 sts with 3¾ mm ndls. Work 6.5 cm (2½ in) in k1, p1 rib.
Change to 4½ mm ndls and work in st st with a panel of 18 sts in ridge patt two in the centre as follows:
Row 1 (right side): K15, p18 as on row 1 of ridge patt two, k15.
Row 2: P15, work 18 as on row 2 of ridge patt two, p15.
Row 3: K15, work 18 as on row 3 of ridge patt two, k15.
Row 4: P15, work 18 as on row 4 of ridge patt two, p15.
Cont thus keeping the centre panel in ridge patt two (beg with row 5 of chart), and the sts at each end in st st as now set, at the same time shape sleeve by inc 1 st at each end of 9th row on chart and afterwards as indicated, still keeping these extra sts in st st and in addition taking 1 extra st at each side of the centre patt panel sts into the ridge patt two on row 11 of chart and afterwards as indicated until there are 72 sts – that is 18 sts at each end in st st and 36 sts in ridge patt two at centre.
Work next 3 rows on chart, taking 1 extra st into ridge patt two at each side of centre panel as indicated on chart.

Now work as follows:
Next row (wrong side – row 68 on chart): Cast on 2 sts, work to end.
Next row (row 69 on chart): Cast on 2 sts, work to end.
Cont working from chart until row 106 has been worked, casting on 2 sts as indicated on chart and keeping these sts in st st and taking 1 extra st into centre patt panel as shown on chart. (Remember the extra turning rows are not indicated on chart.)
There are now 128 sts altogether – that is 36 sts at each end in st st and 56 sts in ridge patt two in centre panel.
Next row (right side – row 107 on chart): Cast on 54 sts (for back side seam), k90, patt 56 in ridge patt two, k36.
Next row (row 108 on chart): Cast on 54 sts (for front side seam), p90, patt 56 in ridge patt two, p90. 236 sts.
Next row (row 109 on chart): P5 as on row 1 of ridge patt one, k83, work 60 sts in ridge patt two, k83, p5 as on row 1 of ridge patt one.
Cont in panels as set beg with row 110 on chart and cont taking 2 extra sts into centre panel of ridge patt two at each side as indicated and at same time take 3 extra sts into ridge patt one as indicated on chart for back and front until row 144 has been worked.

**Divide for neck opening**
(Row 145 on chart): Patt 118 sts and slip these sts on to a st-holder for back. Cont across rem 118 sts for front as follows: cast on 10 sts for stand-up collar and keep these sts in ridge patt two as for yoke and work 30 rows over these 128 sts, but omit the turning rows on ridge patt two between rows 169–178 only to achieve a smooth finish at the centre front.
When the 30 rows have been worked divide for collar opening thus:
Next row (row 175 on chart): Cast off 10 sts, return st on right-hand ndl back on to left-hand ndl, then

cast on 10 sts (collar opening), work to end of row. 128 sts.
Work 29 rows more keeping continuity of patterns. Row 204 on chart has now been worked. Leave these sts on a st-holder.
Return to the 118 sts on first st-holder for back and work as follows:
With wrong side of work facing, rejoin yarn to neck edge and cast on 10 sts for collar back and cont over these 128 sts as on chart for 59 rows (row 204 has now been worked).
Now join the two sets of sts tog as follows:
Next row (row 205 on chart): Patt across the first 118 sts of back, then cast off the last 10 sts (side edge of collar), fasten off, then with the ndl holding the back sts just worked cast off the first 10 sts of front (side edge of front of collar), then patt across last 118 sts of front. (236 sts altogether).
Cont in patt across all these sts, working shapings as indicated on chart until row 240 has been worked.
Cast off 54 sts at beg of next 2 rows, then shape right sleeve as indicated on chart and work one st less each side of centre ridge patt panel as on chart until row 348 has been worked. (48 sts rem – that is 18 sts in centre panel and 15 sts each side in st st).
Change to 3¾ mm ndls and work 6.5 cm (2½ in) in k1, p1 rib. Cast off in rib.

## To Make Up

Do not press. Join side and sleeve seams, using a fine backstitch. Join short sides of stand-up collar with flat seams each side of neck on wrong side.

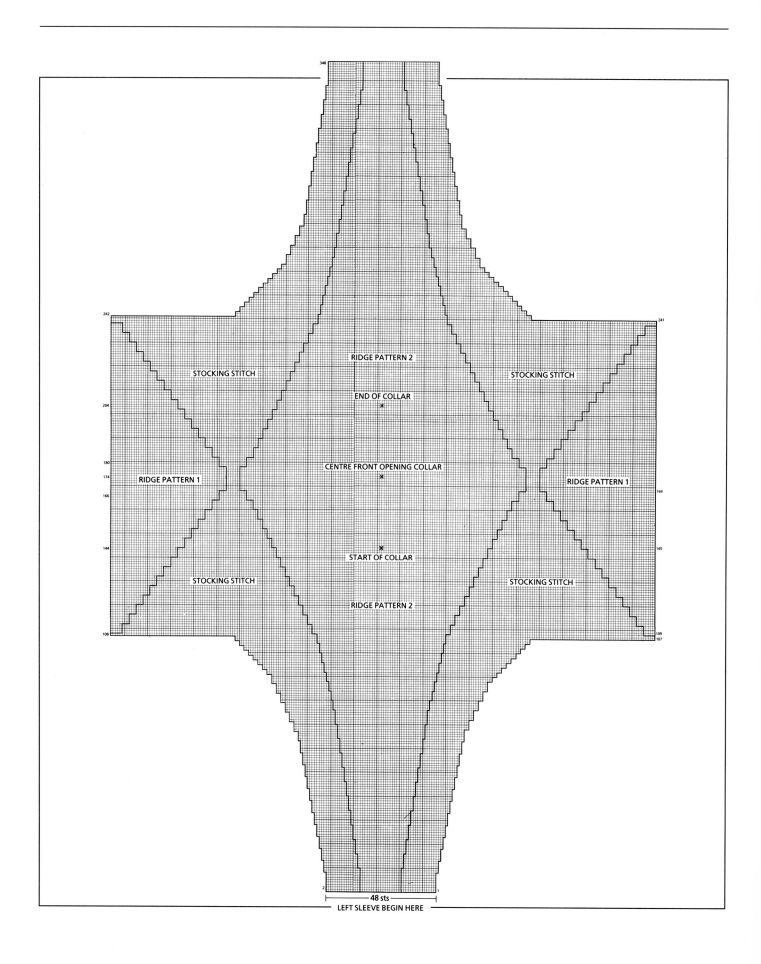

## Stitches used

Mainly in moss stitch. Narrow bands of stocking stitch.

## Sizes

Small/medium/large – to suit bust sizes 86/91/96 cm (34/36/38 in); length from shoulder 67.5 cm (26½ in); sleeve seam 40.5/42/43 cm (16/16½/17 in).

## Materials

Fifteen/sixteen/seventeen 50g balls of Yarnworks Merino Sport; two large buttons; pair of shoulder pads. The quantities of yarn specified are based on average requirements and are therefore approximate.

## Needles

5 mm (no. 6).

## Tension

17 sts and 30 rows to 10 cm (4 in) square measured over moss stitch on 5 mm ndls.

## Note

It is very important that you check your tension carefully before you begin this design. The tension of the knitting controls the size of the finished garment. If your sample has less sts than our tension, try again with smaller ndls and vice versa, then work the garment with the ndls which produce our tension.

## *Instructions*

### BACK

With 5 mm ndls cast on 79/85/91 sts. Work 5 rows in st st, beg and ending with a k row. Still using 5 mm ndls cont in m-st as follows:
*Moss-st row:* K1, * p1, k1; rep from * to end.
Continue in m-st until back measures 43 cm (17 in) from cast-on edge.

### Shape armholes

Cast off 4 sts at beg of next 2 rows, then dec 1 st at each end of next row and every alt row until 57/63/69 sts rem.

Cont straight in m-st until back measures 67.5 cm (26½ in) from cast-on edge.
Cast off straight across.

**RIGHT FRONT**

With 5 mm ndls cast on 53/57/61 sts.
Work 5 rows in st st, beg and ending with a k row.
Work one row in m-st, then cont as follows:
*Row 7:* Sl 1 knitwise, k2 tog (for front slope dec), * p1, k1; rep from * to end.
*Row 8:* * K1, p1; rep from * ending last rep with p1 tbl, instead of p1.
*Row 9:* Sl 1 knitwise, * k1, p1; rep from * to last st, k1.
*Row 10:* As row 8.
*Row 11:* As row 9.
*Row 12:* * K1, p1 rep from * ending last rep with p1, tbl, instead of p1.
*Row 13* (1st buttonhole row): Sl 1 knitwise, p2 tog (for front slope), k1, p1, cast off 5 sts, (1 st on ndl) m-st 11, cast off 5 sts, m-st to end.
*Row 14* (2nd buttonhole row): K1, * p1, k1; rep from * to cast off sts, cast on 5 sts over those cast off to complete the buttonhole, m-st 12, cast on 5 sts over those cast off, then p1, k1, p1, p1 tbl.
*Row 15:* Sl 1 knitwise, * p1, k1; rep from * to end.
*Row 16:* * K1, p1; rep from * to last st, p1 tbl.
*Row 17:* Sl 1 knitwise, * p1, k1; rep from * to end.
*Row 18:* As row 16.
*Row 19:* Sl 1 knitwise, k2 tog (for front slope), * p1, k1; rep from * to end.
*Row 20:* * K1, p1; rep from * ending last rep with p1 tbl, instead of p1.
*Row 21:* Sl 1 knitwise, * k1, p1; rep from * ending last rep with k1.
*Row 22:* As row 20.
*Row 23:* As row 21.
*Row 24:* As row 20.
*Row 25:* Sl 1 knitwise, p2 tog (for front slope), * k1, p1; rep from * to last st, k1.
*Row 26:* * K1, p1; rep from * to last st, p1 tbl.
Cont in m-st decreasing for front slope as before on every 6th row foll last front slope dec until 32/36/40 sts rem, when work should measure about 43 cm (17 in) from cast-on edge (same as back) and ending at side edge.

### ** Shape armhole

Cast off 4 sts (armhole edge) at beg of next row, then dec 1 st at armhole edge of next row and foll 6 alt rows, *at the same time* still decreasing for front slope (as before) on every 6th row foll previous front slope dec. 19/23/27 sts. Keeping armhole edge straight, cont to dec for front slope as before, until 12/15/18 sts rem.
Cont straight until work measures 67.5 cm (26½ in) from cast-on edge.
Cast off.

## LEFT FRONT

With 5 mm ndls cast on 53/57/61 sts.

Work 5 rows in st st, beg and ending with a k row.

Work 2 rows in m-st, then cont as follows:

*Row 8*: Sl 1 knitwise, * p1, k1; rep from * to end.

*Row 9*: * K1, p1; rep from * to last 3 sts, k2 tog tbl (for front slope dec), p1 tbl.

*Row 10*: Sl 1 knitwise, * k1, p1; rep from * to last st, k1.

*Row 11*: * K1, p1; rep from * ending last rep with p1 tbl, instead of p1.

*Row 12*: As row 10.

*Row 13*: As row 11.

*Row 14*: As row 10.

*Row 15*: * K1, p1; rep from * to last 4 sts, k1, p2 tog tbl (for front slope), p1 tbl.

Cont in m-st decreasing for front slope on every 6th row foll previous front slope dec until 32/36/40 sts rem.

Work one row back to side edge when work should measure about 43 cm (17 in) from cast-on edge.

Now work from ** on right front to end.

## SLEEVES (both alike)

With 5 mm ndls cast on 39/41/41 sts.

Work 5 rows in st st, beg and ending with a k row.

Cont in m-st and work 7 rows straight, then inc 1 st at each end of next row and every following 8th row, until there are 61/63/65 sts.

Cont straight until sleeve measures 40.5/42/43 cm (16/16½/17 in) from cast-on edge.

**Shape top**

Cast off 4 sts at beg of next 2 rows. Work 2 rows straight, then dec 1 st at each end of next row and every foll 4th row until 43/45/47 sts rem. Work 2 rows straight, then dec 1 st at each end of next row and every foll 3rd row, until 31/33/35 sts rem. Work one row straight, then dec 1 st at each end of next row and every foll alt row, until 19/19/19 sts rem.

Work 6 rows straight. Cast off.

*To Make Up*

Do not press. Join shoulder seams, using a fine backstitch. Make a pleat at top of sleeves by folding each corner back for 2.5 cm (1 in) and catch-st in place.

Set sleeves into armholes, then join sleeve and side seams, using a fine backstitch.

Sew 2 buttons to left front to correspond with buttonholes. Allow first 5 rows of st st at lower edge of back, fronts and sleeves to roll to the right side.

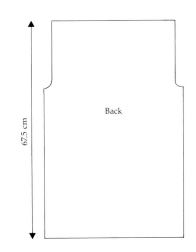

Back

67.5 cm

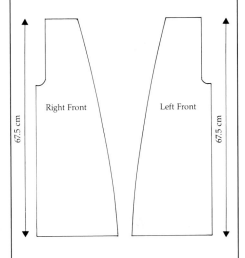

67.5 cm

Right Front

Left Front

67.5 cm

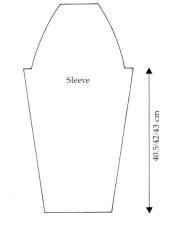

Sleeve

40.5/42/43 cm

# Piecemeal

DOLMAN-SLEEVED SWEATER KNITTED ALL IN ONE PIECE USING TWO DIFFERENT YARNS

## Stitches used
Mainly in stocking stitch. K2, p2 rib for welt, neckband and cuffs.

## Sizes
Small/medium/large – to suit bust sizes 86/91/97 cm (34/36/38 in); length from shoulder 60 cm (23½ in); sleeve seam 36/38/40 cm (14¼/15/15¾ in).

## Materials
Sixteen/sixteen/seventeen 25g balls of Yarnworks Shaggy Dog; three/three/three 50g balls of Yarnworks French Poodle.
These quantities of yarn specified are based on average requirements and are therefore approximate.

## Needles
4½ mm (no. 7); 6½ mm (no. 3) circular ndl 100 cm long; set of four 4 mm (no. 8) double pointed needles (for neckband).

## Tension
13 sts and 17 rows to 10 cm (4 in) square measured over Shaggy Dog on 6½ mm ndls.

## Note
Use a separate length of yarn for each section and twist yarns around each other at back of work when changing yarns to avoid a hole.
Instructions given for three sizes.
This sweater is knitted in one piece on a circular needle working backwards and forwards.

## Special abbreviations
M – Shaggy Dog; C – French Poodle.

## Instructions

### FRONT

With 4½ mm ndls and M, cast on 64/68/72 sts and work 10 cm (4 in) in k2, p2 rib, ending with a wrong-side row.
Change to 6½ mm circular ndl and work backwards and forwards in patt as follows:
*Row 1* (right side): K42/46/50M, 22C.
*Row 2*: P to end in colours as set.
*Row 3*: K41/45/49M, 23C.
*Row 4*: P to end in colours as set.
*Row 5*: K40/44/48M, 24C.
*Row 6*: P to end in colours as set.
Rep the last 2 rows 4 times more.

**Shape sleeves**
*Row 15*: Inc 1, k39/43/47M, 23C, inc 1.
*Row 16*: P24C, 42/46/50M.
*Row 17*: K to end in colours as set.
*Row 18*: P to end in colours as set.
*Row 19*: Inc 1, k41/45/49M, 23C, inc 1.
*Row 20*: P to end in colours as set.
*Row 21*: K44/48/52M, 24C.
*Row 22*: P to end in colours as set.
*Row 23*: Inc 1, k2M, 5C, 37/41/45M, 22C, inc 1.
*Row 24*: P24C, 35/39/43M, 9C, 2M.
*Row 25*: K1M, 11C, 35/39/43M, 23C.
*Row 26*: P23C, 33/37/41M, 14C.
*Row 27*: Inc 1, k14C, 33/37/41M, 21C, inc 1.
*Row 28*: P23C, 32/36/40M, 17C.
*Row 29*: K17C, 33/37/41M, 22C.
*Row 30*: Inc 1, p21C, 32/36/40M, 17C, inc 1.
*Row 31*: K20C, 32/36/40M, 22C.
*Row 32*: P20C, 33/37/41M, 21C.
*Row 33*: Inc 1, k21C, 34/38/42M, 17C, inc 1.
*Row 34*: P17C, 35/39/43M, 24C.
*Row 35*: K24C, 37/41/45M, 11C, 4M.
*Row 36*: Inc 1, p8M, 4C, 38/42/46M, 24C, inc 1.
*Row 37*: K26C, 52/56/60M.
*Row 38*: P51/55/59M, 27C.
*Row 39*: Inc 1, k26C, 50/54/58M, inc 1.

*Row 40*: P to end in colours as set.
*Row 41*: Inc 1, k28C, 50/54/58M, inc 1.
*Row 42*: P to end in colours as set.
*Row 43*: Inc 1, k29C, 51/55/59M, inc 1.
*Row 44*: P52/56/60M, 32C.
*Row 45*: Inc 1, k31C, 51/55/59M, inc 1.
*Row 46*: P to end in colours as set.
*Row 47*: Inc 1, k32C, 52/56/60M, inc 1.
*Row 48*: P55/59/63M, 33C.
*Row 49*: Inc 1, k32C, 54/58/62M, inc 1. 90/94/98 sts.
*Row 50*: P to end in colours as set.
*Row 51*: With M, cast on 4 sts, k4M, 33C, 57/61/65M.
*Row 52*: With M, cast on 4 sts, p4M, 57/61/65M, 33C, 4M. 98/102/106 sts.
*Row 53*: With M, cast on 4 sts, k8M, 33C, 61/65/69M.
*Row 54*: With M, cast on 4 sts, p66/70/74M, 31C, 9M. 106/110/114 sts.
*Row 55*: With M, cast on 4 sts, k13M, 31C, 66/70/74M.
*Row 56*: With M, cast on 4 sts, p71/75/79M, 29C, 14M. 114/118/122 sts.
*Row 57*: With M, cast on 4 sts, k18M, 29C, 71/75/79M.
*Row 58*: With M, cast on 4 sts, p76/80/84M, 27C, 19M. 122/126/130 sts.
*Row 59*: With M, cast on 4 sts, k24M, 25C, 77/81/85M.
*Row 60*: With M, cast on 4 sts, p82/86/90M, 23C, 25M. 130/134/138 sts.
*Row 61*: With M, cast on 4/8/12 sts, k30/34/38M, 21C, 46/50/54M, 5C, 32M.
*Row 62*: With M, cast on 4/8/12 sts, p34/38/42M, 9C, 45/49/53M, 19C, 31/35/39M. 138/150/162 sts.
*Row 63*: K31/35/39M, 19C, 44/48/52M, 11C, 33/37/41M.
*Row 64*: P31/35/39M, 15C, 43/47/51M, 17C, 32/36/40M.
*Row 65*: K33/37/41M, 15C, 43/47/51M, 17C, 30/34/38M.
*Row 66*: P28/32/36M, 19C, 45/49/53M, 11C, 35/39/43M.
*Row 67*: K36/40/44M, 9C, 45/49/53M, 21C, 27/31/35M.

121

Row 68: P26/30/34M, 23C, 46/50/54M, 5C, 38/42/46M.
Row 69: K88/96/104M, 25C, 25/29/33M.
Row 70: P24/28/32M, 27C, 87/95/103M.
Row 71: K86/94/102M, 29C, 23/27/31M.
Row 72: P to end in colours as set.

### Shape neck

Next row: K64/70/76, turn and leave rem sts on a spare needle.
Dec one st at beg of next and every foll alt row neck edge until 59/65/71 sts rem.
Work 3 rows straight. Break off yarn and leave these sts for the present.
Return to sts on spare needle; with right side facing sl first 10 sts on to a holder for neckband, rejoin M to neck edge, k11/13/15M, 31C, 22/26/30M.
Row 74: P to last 2 sts in colours as set, dec 1.
Row 75: K9/11/13M, 33C, 21/25/29M.
Row 76: P to last 2 sts in colours as set, dec 1.
Row 77: K8/10/12M, 33C, 21/25/29M.
Row 78: P20/24/28M, 35C, 5/7/9M, dec 1.
Row 79: K to end in colours as set.
Row 80: P to last 2 sts in colours as set, dec 1.
Row 81: K4/6/8M, 37C, 19/23/27M.
Row 82: P to last 2 sts in colours as set, dec 1.
Row 83: K to end in colours as set.
Row 84: P to end in colours as set.
Row 85: K4/6/8M, 35C, 20/24/28M.

### Join pieces for back

Row 86: P to end in colours as set, cast on 20 sts for back of neck, then with wrong side facing and M, p to

end across sts which were left. 138/150/162 sts.
Row 87: K to end in colours as set.
Row 88: P21/25/29M, 33C, 84/92/100M.
Row 89: K to end in colours as set.
Row 90: P to end in colours as set.
Row 91: K85/93/101M, 31C, 22/26/30M.
Row 92: P to end in colours as set.
Row 93: K86/94/102M, 29C, 23/27/31M.
Row 94: P to end in colours as set.
Row 95: K87/95/103M, 27C, 24/28/32M.
Row 96: P25/29/33M, 25C, 88/96/104M.
Row 97: K88/96/104M, 24C, 26/30/34M.
Row 98: P27/31/35M, 22C, 31/35/39M, 5C, 53/57/61M.
Row 99: K51/55/59M, 9C, 29/33/37M, 21C, 28/32/36M.
Row 100: P29/33/37M, 19C, 29/33/37M, 11C, 50/54/58M.
Row 101: K48/52/56M, 15C, 27/31/35M, 19C, 29/33/37M.
Row 102: P30/34/38M, 17C, 27/31/35M, 17C, 47/51/55M.
Row 103: K47/51/55M, 18C, 27/31/35M, 15C, 31/35/39M.
Row 104: P33/37/41M, 11C, 29/33/37M, 19C, 46/50/54M.
Row 105: K45/49/53M, 21C, 29/33/37M, 9C, 34/38/42M.
Row 106: P36/40/44M, 5C, 30/34/38M, 23C, 44/48/52M.
Row 107: K44/48/52M, 24C, 70/78/86M.
Row 108: P69/77/85M, 26C, 43/47/51M.

### Shape sleeves

Row 109: Cast off 4/8/12 sts, k38M, including st on right needle 28C, 68/76/84M.
Row 110: Cast off 4/8/12 sts, p to end in colours as set. 130/134/138 sts.
Row 111: Cast off 4 sts, k33M, 30C, 63/67/71M.
Row 112: Cast off 4 sts, p to end in colours as set. 122/126/130 sts.
Row 113: Cast off 4 sts, k28M, 32C, 58/62/66M.
Row 114: Cast off 4 sts, p to end in colours as set. 114/118/122 sts.

Row 115: Cast off 4 sts, k to end in colours as set.
Row 116: Cast off 4 sts, p49/53/57M, 34C, 23M. 106/110/114 sts.
Row 117: Cast off 4 sts, k to end in colours as set.
Row 118: Cast off 4 sts, p to end in colours as set. 98/102/106 sts.
Row 119: Cast off 4 sts, k14M, 36C, 44/48/52M.
Row 120: Cast off 4 sts, p to end in colours as set. 90/94/98 sts.
Row 121: Dec 1, k12M, 36C, 38/42/46M, dec 1.
Row 122: P to end in colours as set.
Row 123: Dec 1, k12M, 34C, 38/42/46M, dec 1.
Row 124: P to end in colours as set.
Row 125: Dec 1, k11M, 34C, 37/41/45M, dec 1.
Row 126: P39/43/47M, 32C, 13M.
Row 127: Dec 1, k11M, 32C, 37/41/45M, dec 1.
Row 128: P to end in colours as set.
Row 129: Dec 1, k11M, 30C, 37/41/45M, dec 1.
Row 130: P to end in colours as set.
Row 131: Dec 1, k11M, 28C, 37/41/45M, dec 1.
Row 132: P to end in colours as set.
Row 133: K13M, 26C, 39/43/47M.
Row 134: Dec 1, p38/42/46M, 24C, 12M, dec 1.
Row 135: K13M, 23C, 40/44/48M.
Row 136: P41/45/49M, 21C, 14M.
Row 137: Dec 1, k13M, 19C, 40/44/48M, dec 1.
Row 138: P to end in colours as set.
Row 139: K15M, 17C, 42/46/50M.
Row 140: Dec 1, p41/45/49M, 15C, 14M, dec 1.
Row 141: K17M, 11C, 44/48/52M.
Row 142: P45/49/53M, 9C, 18M.
Row 143: Dec 1, k18M, 5C, 45/49/53M, dec 1.
Cont in M only, work 3 rows straight.
Dec one st at each end of next and every foll 4th row until 64/68/72 sts rem.
Cont without shaping until back measures the same as front to top of welt, ending with a p row.
Change to 4½ mm ndls and work 10 cm (4 in) in k2, p2 rib.
Cast off in rib.

## CUFFS

With 4½ mm ndls, M and right side facing, pick up and k 36 sts evenly along sleeve edge and work 7 cm (2¾ in) in k2, p2 rib.
Cast off in rib.

## NECKBAND

With set of four 4 mm ndls, M and right side facing, pick up and k 19 sts evenly down left front neck, k10 front neck sts from holder, then pick up and k 19 sts evenly up right front neck and 24 sts across back neck. 72 sts.
Work 8 rounds in k2, p2 rib.
Cast off loosely in rib.

## To Make Up

Do not press. Join side and sleeve seams with matching thread, using a fine backstitch.

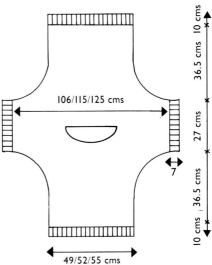

106/115/125 cms

10 cms

36.5 cms

27 cms

36.5 cms

10 cms

7

49/52/55 cms

# Blue-blooded

## Stitches used
Mainly in stocking stitch. K2, p2 rib for welt, collar, cuffs and inset.

## Sizes
Small/medium/large – to suit bust sizes 86/91/97 cm (34/36/38 in); length from shoulder 66 cm (26 in); sleeve seam 38/41/44 cm (15/16¼/17¼ in).

## Materials
Twenty/twenty-one/twenty-two 25g balls of Yarnworks Shaggy Dog Sparkle; 2 shoulder pads. The quantities of yarn specified are based on average requirements and are therefore approximate.

## Needles
4½ mm (no. 7); 6½ mm (no. 3); 6½ mm circular ndl 100 cm long; set of four 4½ mm and 5½ mm (no. 5) double pointed needles.

## Tension
13 sts and 17 rows to 10 cm (4 in) square measured over st st on 6½ mm ndls.

## Note
Instructions given for three sizes. This sweater is knitted in one piece.

## Instructions

### LOWER FRONT

With 4½ mm ndls cast on 64/68/72 sts, using thumb method as shown.
Work in k2, p2 rib for 18 cm (7 in).
Change to 6½ mm ndls.
Beg with a k row, cont in st st until work measures 25 cm (10 in) from beg, ending with a p row.

### Divide for front 'V'
*Next row*: K32/34/36, turn and leave rem sts on a spare needle.
*Next row*: P to end.

### Shape sleeve
*Next row*: Inc 1, k to last 2 sts, skpo.
Work 3 rows straight.
Rep the last 4 rows twice more.
*Next row*: Inc 1, k to last 2 sts, skpo.
Work 2 rows straight.
*Next row*: P2 tog tbl, p to last st, inc 1.
Work 2 rows straight.
Rep the last 6 rows once more.
*Next row*: Inc 1, k to last 2 sts, skpo.
*Next row*: P to end.
*Next row*: Inc 1, k to end.
*Next row*: P2 tog tbl, p to end.
*Next row*: Inc 1, k to end.
*Next row*: P to end.
Rep the last 6 rows once more.
Cont to dec one st at front edge on next and every foll 3rd row as set, *at the same time*, cast on 4 sts at beg of next and foll 5/6/7 alt rows. 54/60/65 sts.
Place a marker side edge of last row.
Keeping sleeve edge straight, cont to dec at front edge until 47/53/59 sts rem.
Cont without shaping until work measures 13 cm (5 in) from marker, ending with a k row. **
Leave these sts for the present.
Return to sts on spare needle; with right side facing, rejoin yarn to front edge and k to end.
Cont to match first side to **, reversing all shapings.

### Join pieces
Change to 6½ mm circular ndl, work backwards and forwards.
*Next row*: P to end, cast on 44 sts loosely for back of neck, then with wrong side facing, p to end across sts which were left. 138/150/162 sts.
Cont in st st until work measures 26 cm (10¼ in) from markers, ending with a p row.

### Shape sides
Cast off 4 sts at beg of next 12/14/16 rows. 90/94/98 sts.
Dec one st at each end of next and every foll alt row until 78/82/86 sts rem, every foll 3rd row until 70/74/78 sts rem, then every foll 4th row until 64/68/72 sts rem.
Cont without shaping until back measures the same as front to top of welt, ending with a p row.
Change to 4½ mm ndls and work 18 cm (7 in) in k2, p2 rib.
Cast off loosely in rib.

### FRONT INSET

With 4½ mm ndls cast on 2 sts.
*Row 1* (right side): P to end.
*Row 2*: K1, (k1, p1) in last st.
*Row 3*: K1, p1, (p1, k1) in last st.
*Row 4*: P1, k2, p twice into last st.
*Row 5*: K2, p2, k twice into last st.
*Row 6*: P2, k2, p1, (p1, k1) in last st.
*Row 7*: P1, k2, p2, k1, (k1, p1) in last st.
Work twice into last st of every row taking extra sts into k2, p2 rib as set, until there are 73 sts, thus ending with a wrong-side row.

### Shape neck
*Row 1*: Rib 30, turn and leave rem sts on a spare needle.
*Row 2 and every foll alt row*: Rib to end, inc 1.
*Row 3*: Rib 29, turn.
*Row 5*: Rib 28, turn.
*Row 7*: Rib 27, turn.
*Row 9*: Rib 26, turn.
*Row 11*: Rib 25, turn.
*Row 12*: As row 2.
Work 10 rows straight in rib on these 26 sts.
Cast off in rib.
With right side facing, sl 10 shaping sts and then first 14 sts on spare needle on to a holder for collar, rejoin yarn to neck edge, rib to last st, inc 1.
Cont to match first side, reversing all shaping.

## CUFFS

With 4½ mm ndls and right side facing, pick up and k 38 sts evenly along sleeve edge.
Work in k2, p2 rib for 7 cm (2¾ in).
Cast off in rib.

## COLLAR

Sew front inset into 'V' shape, sewing 26 cast-off sts at either side to cast-on sts at back neck but leaving centre 18 sts free for collar. With set of four 4½ mm needles and right side facing, sl first 17 sts from holder on to spare needle thus beg at centre front neck, p1, (k2, p2) 4 times across rem sts on holder and shaping sts of right front neck, pick up and k 10 sts evenly up right front neck, 26 sts across back neck and 10 sts down left front neck, (p2, k2) 4 times, p1 across sts on spare needle, turn. 80 sts.
Work backwards and forwards as follows.
Work 4 rows in rib as set.
Change to set of four 5½ mm needles and work 9 more rows.
Cast off loosely in rib.

## To Make Up

Do not press. Join side and sleeve seams, using a fine back stitch.
Sew in shoulder pads.

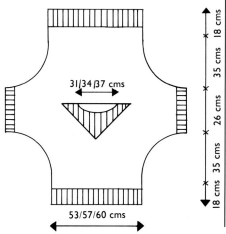

Write to the addresses below for details of mail order, enclosing a stamped addressed envelope.

**GREAT BRITAIN**
Woolly Ideas,
46 City Road,
Cambridge,
Cambs. CB1 1DP
Tel: 0223-312574

Colourworks,
23 Regent Street,
Cheltenham,
Glos. GL50 1HE
Tel: 0242-570243

Wellington Wools,
Unit 2,
Wellington Centre,
Aldershot,
Hants. GU11 1DB
Tel: 0252-317111

The Wool Works,
48 Friar Street,
Worcester,
Hereford & Worcs. WR1 2NA
Tel: 0905-29228

Broadbents of Southport Ltd,
19 Chapel Street,
Southport,
Lancs. PR8 1AR
Tel: 0704-35252

Harrods Ltd,
87 Brompton Road,
Knightsbridge,
London SW1X 7XL
Tel: 01-730-1234

K1 P1,
174 Northcote Road,
London SW11
Tel: 01-228-5806

Liberty plc,
Regent Street,
London W1R 6AH
Tel: 01-734-1234

Fenwick Ltd,
Brent Cross Shopping Centre,
Hendon,
London NW4 3FN
Tel: 01-202-8200

Susan Murray,
84 Victoria Street,
Edinburgh,
Lothian. EH1 2HG
Tel: 031-226-2532

Knit It,
435 Richmond Road,
Twickenham,
Middx. TW1 2EF
Tel: 01-891-0772

Parc Laine,
9 Little Clarendon Street,
Oxford OX1 2HP
Tel: 0865-516239

Catherine Parr,
26 Duke Street,
Henley-upon-Thames,
Oxon. RG9 1UP
Tel: 0491-573320

Antony Sheppard Ltd,
Papyrus Warehouse,
Pentrerhedyn Street,
Machynlleth,
Powys. SY20 8DJ
Tel: 0654-2344

Cloud Nine,
15 Sheep Street,
Skipton,
N. Yorks. BD23 1JH
Tel: 0756-69594

Woolies (GW) Ltd,
81 High Street,
Gosforth,
Newcastle-upon-Tyne,
Tyne & Wear. NE3 4AA
Tel: 0632-852848

Osa,
11/12 The Parade,
St. Mary's Place,
Shrewsbury,
Salop.
Tel: 0743-55533

Siop Jen,
36/38 Castle Arcade,
Cardiff,
South Glamorgan CF1 2BW
Tel: 0222-42933

Handi Wools,
15 Church Street,
Calne,
Wilts.
Tel: 0249-812081

Stitches,
Dovehouse Parade,
355 Warwick Road,
Solihull,
W. Midlands
Tel: 021-706-1048

In case of difficulty obtaining
  yarns, please contact:
Liz Gavaghan,
Customer Relations Dept,
Yarnworks Ltd,
Albert Mills,
Horbury,
Nr. Wakefield,
W. Yorks.
Tel: 0924-278206

**USA**
* Denotes companies which
  supply yarn mail order

Memory Haglar,
2031 Canyon Rd,
Birmingham,
Alabama 35216

In Stitches,
5E Figueron St,
Santa Barbara,
California 93101

Greenwich Yarns,
2073 Greenwich St,
San Francisco,
California 94123

Aspen Wool Company,
520 E Durant,
Aspen,
Colorado 81611

The Knit Shop,
118 East Tarpon Ave,
Tarpon Springs,
Florida 33589

Weaving Workshop,
916 West Diversey Parkway,
Chicago,
Illinois 60614*

Needle Antics,
2515 East 65 St,
Indianapolis,
Indiana 46220

Creative Corner,
332 Fifth St,
Des Moines,
Iowa 50265

Martha Hall,
46 Main St,
Yarmouth,
Maine*

Outrageous Yarns,
170 Newbury St,
Boston,
Massachusetts

Tanglewool,
57 Church St,
Lenox,
Massachusetts 01240*

Wild and Wooly,
1800 Massachusetts Ave,
Lexington,
Massachusetts 02173*

Knitworks Inc,
5221 South 48 St,
Lincoln,
Nebraska 68516*

Whistles,
5 Beechwood Rd,
Summit,
New Jersey 07901

Coultar Studios,
118 East 59 St,
New York,
NY 10022*

Stitch in Time Studios,
2101 Richmond Rd,
Beechwood,
Ohio 44122

Knotting Chamber,
3257 SE Hawthorne,
Portland,
Oregon 97214

The Wooly West,
Salt Lake City,
Utah 84172

Knitting Basket,
5812 Grove Ave,
Richmond,
Virginia 23226*

Marie's Wild and Wooly,
17791 Fjord Drive, NE,
Poulses,
Washington 98370

## CANADA
Write to the address of the
  distributor for stockist
  information.
Calana,
544 Schoolhouse Street,
Coquitlam,
Vancouver,
British Columbia V3J 5P1

## AUSTRALIA
Contact the address below for
  mail order.
Knitting Wool Centre,
6 Royal Arcade,
Melbourne,
Victoria
Tel: Melbourne 654 7890

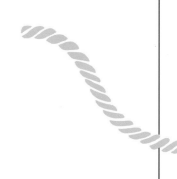